P

MW01180545

CUBA

1994

Hayit Publishing

1st Edition 1994

ISBN 1-874251-17-7
© copyright 1994 original version: Hayit Verlag GmbH,
Cologne/Germany

Author: Ole Helmhausen
Translation, Adaption, Revision: Scott Reznik
Assistant Editor: Sabarah Hanif
Typesetting: Hayit Publishing
Print :Druckhaus Cramer, Greven/Germany
Cover Photo: Ole Helmhausen
Back Cover Photos: Nicolai Blechinger
Photos:
      Nicolai Blechinger: p. 27
      Jürgen Bugler: p. 30, 63
      Cubatur: p. 11, 98
      Ole Helmhausen: p.7, 23, 35, 58, 70, 74, 78, 86, 90, 106,
      111,114, 118, 123, 126
      Volkmar E. Janicke: p. 110, 119
      Maps: Ralf Sausen, Ralf Tito

2.6/Rs/Tu

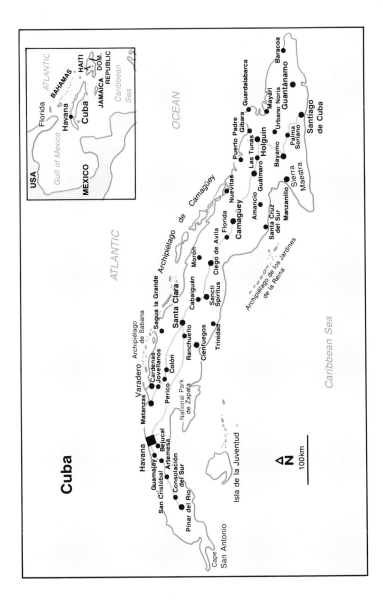

Using this book

Books in the *Practical Travel* series offer a wealth of practical information. You will find the most important tips for your travels conveniently arranged in alphabetical order. Cross-references aid in orientation so that even entries which are not covered in depth, for instance "Holiday Apartments", lead you to the appropriate entry, in this case "Accommodation" Also thematically altered entries are cross-referenced. For example under the heading "Medication", there appear the following references: "Medical Care", "Pharmacies", "Vaccinations".

With travel guides from the *Practical Travel* series, the information is already available before you depart on your trip. Thus, you are already familiar with necessary travel documents and maps, even customs regulations. Travel within the country is made easier through comprehensive presentation of public transportation, car rentals in addition to the practical tips ranging from medical assistance to newspapers available in the country. The descriptions of cities are arranged alphabetically as well and include the most important facts about the particular city, its history and a summary of significant sights. In addition, these entries include a wealth of practical tips - from shopping, restaurants and accommodation to important local addresses. Background information does not come up short either. You will find interesting information about the people and their culture as well as the regional geography, history and current political and economic situation.

Cuba - a Caribbean pearl

A favourite destination with sun-hungry travellers, this island has grown in popularity for a holiday on the beach. Even in January and February

when the water temperature "plummets" to 24°C (75°F), visitors flock to the beaches - and they'll have the beaches all to themselves during this time of year since Cubans consider it much too cold... Sand as white as sugar, crystal clear water - not only the beautiful island of Cayo Largo offers this setting.

The diversity of landscapes will also meet with the satisfaction of those who aren't only out to sunbathe: extensive plains and rolling hills characterise the island's profile. The Sierra Maestra draws visitors into this region, where remnants of tropical vegetation have managed to endure on the northern slopes of this mountain chain. Add to this more than 6,000 kilometres (3,750 miles) of coastline where not only the snow-white beaches but the rugged coastal cliff formations hold an attraction all their own. Numerous reservoirs which catch the water from the swelling rivers during the rainy season augment these impressions of Cuba.

Cuba's cultural aspects, based heavily on Spanish and African influences, also add to these Caribbean impressions. Cities with a dynamic past and present await those wishing to discover Cuba culturally. It was not by mere chance that Graham Greene and Ernest Hemingway were so enchanted with this island. Some visitors will certainly want to retrace their steps here. Many others come to Cuba during the summer to celebrate Carnival in a flood of colour.

And no matter what time of year one visits this Caribbean pearl, one should definitely sample a daiquiri at the "Floridita" in Havana, one of Hemingway's favourites. Cuban cuisine will prove to be a culinary delight: good food and plenty of it, with numerous specialities on the menus in restaurants. Be sure to try "moros y christianos"Moors and Christians) Cuba's national dish.

Contents

Registry of Places

Baconao 9
Banes 9
Baracoa 9
Batabanó 11
Bayamo 12
Bay of Pigs 12
Camagüey 14
Cardenas 19
Cayo Largo 19
Ciego de Avila 20
Cienfuegos 20
Cojimar 25
El Cobre 34
Gibara 37
Gran Piedra National Park
and La Isabelica 38
Granjita Siboney 38
Guamá 39
Guanahacabibes 39
Guantánamo 40
Guardalavaca 40
Hanabanilla 41
Havana 41
Holguín 79
La Guira National Park 82
Mariel 83
Matanzas 83
Pinar del Río 88
Sancti Spíritus 92
Santa Clara 93
Santa Lucía 94
Santiago de Cuba 97
Soroa 107
Trinidad 116
Varadero 121
Viñales 128

General Information

Accommodation 7
Animals and Wildlife 8
Business Hours 14
Car Rental 18
Climate 24
Clothing and Equipment 25
Crime 26
Cuisine 26
Cultural Institutions 31
Currency 31
Currency Exchange and
Regulations 31
Customs Regulations 32
Economy 33
Electricity 34
Embassies and Consulates 36
Geography 36
History 67
Holidays and Celebrations 80
Language 82
Literature 82
Maps 82
Markets 83
Medical Care 84
Music 85
Nudism 85
People 85
Photography 87
Politics and Government 91
Religion 91
Shopping 105
Sights 107
Telephones 108
Tipping 108
Tourist Season 108
Traffic Regulations 108
Travel Documents 109
Travel in Cuba 110
Travelling to Cuba 115
Vegetation 127

Accommodation

The larger tourist hotels are suitable for those tourists from western industrialised nations. There are mainly newly built luxurious houses here. Room
reservations can be booked with *Cubatur (→ Travelling in Cuba/Cubatur and
Intur)*. A five star rating means a high international standard and it costs around
$60/35 a night. Most of the hotels recommended in this travel guide have a
2 or 3 star rating. For the most part, rooms are equipped with a bath, a toilet
and air conditioning. A restaurant, a bar and a swimming pool are also part of
the setup.
After checking in the guests receive a hotel card, called "Tarjeta de Huesped".
The name, room number and the checking in date of the guests is marked on
these cards. This card must be carried by the guests at all times and be shown
when the guest wants to use the hotel's restaurant, bar or swimming pool. It
should not be left by the guests in their rooms. Check out time is at around 2
pm.
At 3 pm rooms are ready to be used again. Dirty laundry can be given to the
maid. However the room prices are for double rooms and do not include meals

*Before the revolution, this was a luxurious villa with a private beach paradise:
today, it is a hotel and the beach is open to the public*

(for meals →*Cuisine*). Apart from these **Hotels** which are almost exclusively frequented by western tourists, there are an immense number of smaller and less expensive hotels. Due to the fact that these hotels are not under *Cubatur,* they must be booked independently. This has become less common in recent times. There are no *Youth Hostels.* Villas and tourist holiday villages are situated on the more popular beaches. These villages offer basic bungalows (cabañas) which have one or two rooms and are also equipped with a restaurant, a bar and a discotheque. They can be booked through Cubatur.
Camping is still in its early stages here. The sanitary conditions are really primitive and the tropical climate (the nights are chilly and the days are burning hot) as well as the changing locations of the campsites, make the camping experience no easy task. The "Instituto Nacional de Turismo" give out information in camping in Cuba. This office is located corner of Malecón y Calle G, La Habana 4.

Animals and Wildlife

Cuba is an island surrounded by waters which are a habitat for around 900 species of fish. Among the most widely-known, edible fish are the *loach* and the *sea bass* as well as the *marlin,* the meat of which is at the top of menus in speciality restaurants. However, eating fish is not at all popular among Cubans. When they had to tighten their belts after the victory of the revolution, the new government appealed to the population in vain for quite a while to eat the inexpensive fish at least once a week. It was only when Fidél Castro himself had fried fish served during a television broadcast, eating it in silence and subsequently declaring that he would eat only fish on television until the nutritional value of fish was understood even in the most remote corner of Cuba that the nation did gradually change its eating habits. In contrast, other aquatic creatures are considered a delicacy: the *crocodile.* These have meanwhile all but disappeared from the swamps and mangrove thickets and can only be seen on the crocodile farms of the marshy Zapata Peninsula. From the crocodile ranch in →*Guamá,* one can take a boat trip over the Laguna del Tesoro, a relatively demanding trip during the midday heat and considering the stench of the diesel fumes. In addition, there are still a few of the legendary sea-cows, the *manatis* living in the waters of this region. They were almost completely wiped out after having been hunted for their meat.
Another rarity is the *manjuari,* a fish with the head of a crocodile – of course not of the same dimensions since this fish is about as large as a pike.
The only larger vertebrate species which one can come across in Cuba are the *Almiqui,* a long-snouted insect eater as well as an animal called *Jutia Conga* similar to a rat. The Almiqui can only still be found in the Oriente and is in danger of becoming extinct. The Jutia Conga already provided the native

Indian population and later the Spanish farmers with a welcome change on their supper tables.

There are over 300 species of birds in Cuba, among them also the world's smallest bird, the *Zunzuncito*. This bird is a distant relative of the domesticated canary and can be found in the mangrove thickets along the coast. Other colourful and elegant birds include the *flamingos* which are found near →*Cienfuegos* on Cuba's southern coast and on the Island of Youth. Less elegant but providing a necessary service are the *black raven vultures,* feeding mainly on carrion as well as the white herons which stick to live animals and make life difficult for the cattle. While one will always come upon these birds in Cuba, two-thirds of the bird species are only on the island for a limited amount of time. These are the migratory birds which stop in Cuba on their way to South America.

Baconao

The Baconao National Park lies in the province of Santiago de Cuba. UNESCO has declared this a nature reserve since this is one of the last areas where the ecosystem is still intact. The park comprises 80,000 hectares (200,000 acres) and includes the mountain "La Gran Piedra", the French coffee plantation "La Isabelica", the botanical gardens, the Santiago zoo, a prehistoric valley, the house where Pedro El Cojo was born as well as several hotels and beaches. →*Gran Piedra National Park.*

Banes

The city of Banes lies in the province of Holguín, only 30 kilometres (19 miles) from the famous beach of →*Guardalavaca*. The city was founded in 1887 and has a population of a little over 85,000 today. This was the site of a large Indian settlement. In a nicely set up museum there are excavated relics, among others stone tools and animal figures in gold, offering an interesting insight into the everyday life of the pre-Colombian Indians of Cuba.

Banks →*Currency Exchange and Regulations*

Baracoa

The city of Baracoa was founded in 1512 and has a population of 50,000 today. It lies around 200 kilometres (125 miles) north east of Santiago de Cuba in the Oriente region to the east. The air here is tropical and humid. Crops harvested here include bananas, coconuts and some coffee. The processing industry is limited here. Tourists seldom wander into the city since it is quite far to the next tourist spot.

Baracoa / **History**

Baracoa is the first Spanish settlement to be founded on Cuban territory as well as being one of the oldest cities to be founded by Europeans on the American continent. The "ciudad primada" served as Cuba's capital during the first three years after it was founded until this function was taken over by →*Santiago de Cuba*. Among other factors the activities of the Indian chief Hatuey also contributed to moving the capital. He led battles against the hated Spaniards with the natives and remained their irreconcilable adversary until his death whereby he was burnt at the stake.

The settlers source of livelihood was fruit, yucca and maize (corn), they also harvested cocoa and coffee. Their affluence, however, remained limited since the "alturas" directly beyond the city impaired agriculture on a large scale. When roads and the railway were later built all over Cuba, Baracoa was simply forgotten behind the mountains. The "ciudad primada" became the "ciudad muerta", the dead city. There was not even a paved road to Guantánamo in existence until 1959. Only with the revolutionary government was this road built which had been promised for so long. "La Farola", as this roadway is called, leads through very beautiful landscape making it a good enough reason to pay a visit to Baracoa.

During the war for independence *(→History)* this region surrounding the city was the site of many historically significant battles. The Mulatto General Antonio Maceo took possession of the city in 1877, under control of the Spaniards at that time. Quite nearby, near the village of Duaba, he then landed once again to battle against the Spaniards after his exile in 1895.

60 years later numerous young people from this region joined the rebels' army under Fidel Castro with enthusiasm.

Baracoa / **Sights**

Matachín Fortress: The Matachín fortress originates from 1802 and lies high above the city. During the war for independence, it served the Spaniards as a lookout. Only a few years ago the Cuban cultural ministry had the fortress completely renovated. Housed in its interior is a small museum of local history.

El Castillo Fortress, also called Seburuco or Sanguily: like the Matachín fortress El Castillo was also laid out to protect the city and the bay; El Castillo now houses the best hotel in the city.

Playitas: Playitas is small and insignificant; the beach however is significant in terms of recent Cuban history and the national pride of its population. On April 11th, 1895, José Martí, the "Apostle of Freedom" *(→History)* along with General Máximo Gomez landed here to confront the Spanish for one last time. Today it is a national monument.

Duaba: Ten days before the above event Antonio Maceo landed at this point to join the rebel forces on April 1st. This is also a national monument.
Placa Indepencia: This is the site where the first church in Cuba was erected.

Baracoa / **Practical Information**
Accommodation: Accommodation can be found in Hotel *El Castillo,* Calle Calixto Garcia (double rooms $34/£20).
Restaurant: In *La Puerta,* on the bay, the cuisine is prepared according to old Cuban recipes.

Batabanó
Where Batabanó is now located was the original site of Havana, Cuba's capital city, 55 kilometres (34 miles) south of its present location on the southern coast west of Cuba. Founded in 1515, Batabanó meanwhile has a population of 15,000 who live predominantly from fishing. For tourists, only the harbour is of any significance. From here, the speedy hydrofoils take passengers over to Isla de la Juventud, a crossing that takes 5 hours by normal ferry.

An especially enjoyable pastime is a leisurely stroll through the historic cities of Cuba

Bay of Pigs

On April 17, 1961, Washington's Central American policy experienced its own Waterloo in the "Bahia de Cochinos" or the "Bay of Pigs." Supported by 24 aircrafts and 14 battleships, troops of exiled Cubans trained by the CIA landed here. After 72 hours of fighting, their attack was, however, fended off. Many bled to death in the swamps but most could be taken prisoner. Along the street from Boca de Guamá (→*Guamá*) to Playa Girón, there are 80 memorial stone markers for the 80 revolutionary fighters who fell in this battle. In the town of Playa Girón is a monument as well as the *Museo de la Intervención,* documenting this key event in Cuban →*History*. Maps show the different phases of the invasion, photos and newspaper articles supplement the documentation. *Cubatur* offers excursions here on a regular basis.

Accommodation: Villa *Playa Girón.* An inexpensive holiday village with a cafeteria, a bar and a swimming pool. Double rooms are priced from $24 (£14).

Bayamo

Bayamo is a beautiful city set against the rugged backdrop of the Sierra Maestra and situated in the cattle breeding region of Cuba. The city was founded in 1513, it has a population of 100,000 and is the capital of the Granma Province. It is 127 kilometres (80 miles) to Santiago de Cuba to the southeast and 841 kilometres (526 miles) to Havana. In addition to cattle breeding, sugar cane, coffee, cocoa and citrus fruits play an important role in the cities economy. Located nearby is the second largest rice producing region at the confluence of the Rio Caúto.

Bayamo / **History**

The residents of Bayamo demonstrated their resistance to the Spanish very early on in the city's history. When, for example, the governor tried to combat the smuggling trade in which everyone was involved from the bishop to the slave, of Bayamo were condemned to death, the residents promptly stormed his envoys residence and freed the prisoners.

During the 18th and 19th centuries the progressive residents of Bayamo founded Masonic temples, of which, "Estrella Tropical" was the most famous. Bayamo was also where the "Bayamesa" was composed and sung for the first time and was later to become the Cuban national anthem. Carlos Manuel de Céspedes also proclaimed The Free Republic of Cuba at the nearby "La Demajagua" farm on October 10th, 1868 and began the first Cuban war of independence, leading an army of freed slaves and the poor farm workers. The residents set fire to the city in order for it not to fall in the hands of the hated Spaniards. Since then, the city has had the proud epithet of "La Héroica", the heroic.

Other key historical events took place quite nearby. In 1895 José Martí fell in one of the first battles in the war for independence near Dos Ríos. On December 6 in 1956, the "Granma" yacht with Fidél Castro, "Che" Guevara and 80 freedom fighters aboard landed near the small town of Niquero on the Playa Colorado.

Bayamo / **Sights**

Casa Natal de Carlos Manuel de Céspedes: The house where the "Padre de la Patria" (Father of the Nation) was born, is situated on Parque Céspedes and is dedicated to this man's life and work. On exhibit here are personal articles and notes written by the noteworthy man Carlos Manuel de Céspedes; in addition, this museum also provides a brief overview of the Cuban wars of independence. The acclaimed epithet was awarded to de Céspedes shortly after the war began when Spanish soldiers imprisoned one of his sons and held him hostage. Céspedes did not give into their demands to lay down their weapons and surrender; instead Céspedes responded that all Cubans were his sons. He, therefore, could not surrender the freedom of all for one individual. His son was then shot and killed.

Iglesia Parroquíal de San Salvador: The national anthem was sung for the first time in the Parroquíal Mayor de San Salvador Church. This church is only one block from Parque Céspedes and can be easily recognised by its yellow façade. As one of the oldest churches in Cuba, the interior has been lovingly furnished. During the 1970s, it was completely renovated and declared a national monument.

The Droschkes of Bayamo: Bayamo's atmosphere can best be discovered during a ride in one of the numerous horse-drawn droshkes ("coches") which are still in existence today. The residents of Bayamo even immortalised this means of transportation in a well-known hit song and still use these to get around town. Vacant "coches" can be stopped along the streets by waving one's hand. There is also a droshke service in the *Sierra Maestra* Hotel.

Museo Histórico La Demajagua: The tourist office in the *Sierra Maestra* Hotel will organise an excursion to the old plantation of La Demajagua near Manzanillo upon request.

It was from this point that the first Cuban war of independence began when Céspedes was the first plantation owner to free his slaves and subsequently declared the Republic of Cuba *(→History)*. Today, this plantation is a national monument and a popular destination for school field trips from the surrounding regions. Tourists only rarely venture off to this area.

Bayamo / **Practical Information**

Accommodation: Hotel *Sierra Maestra,* Carretera Central on the road to Santiago de Cuba. A modern tourist hotel with double rooms starting at $34 (£20).

Hotel *Royalton,* Parque de Céspedes. A hotel with a lot of atmosphere but somewhat neglected. Centrally located.

Restaurants: One good restaurant can be found in *Sierra Maestra.* Inexpensive places to eat are located in the side-streets surrounding Parque Céspedes.

Beverages →*Cuisine*
Buses → *Travel in Cuba and individuel entries*

Business Hours

All offices, including the Cubatur offices are generally open Monday to Friday from 8:30 am to 5:30 pm. The lunch break however, varies greatly. One could find oneself before closed doors during business hours. The "merienda" is, however, usually between 12:30 and 1:30 pm. Every second Saturday in the month, the Cubans work until noon.

Post offices are open Monday to Saturday from 8 am to 10 pm and Sundays from 8 am to 6 pm.

Cinemas in Havana begin their showings around 5 pm and close around midnight.

Museums are generally open only during the afternoon. Their main hours are from 2 to 7 pm. They are also open during the morning hours on Sundays and remain closed all day Mondays.

Shops and stores are open Monday to Saturday from 9:30 to 12:30 and from 3 to 7 pm. Many stores in Havana first open at 12:30 and close at 7:30 pm. Every second Saturday is a day off for the Cubans.

Camagüey

With a population of 250,000 Camagüey is the third largest city in Cuba, situated in a region of lush, tropical vegetation. The area is extensive and flat, making it ideal for cattle breeding. The Camagüey region is one of the most sparsely populated in Cuba. It is around 571 kilometres (357 miles) to Havana and 398 kilometres (249 miles) to Santiago de Cuba. Thanks to its elegant palaces from the colonial period, Camagüey is among the most beautiful cities on the island. The economy is still based on cattle breeding and the production of sugar. During the 1960s, the fish processing industry in Nuevitas to the north has also become an economic factor for this city.

Camagüey / **History**

The Camagüeyanos have always been characterised by their initiative and decisiveness. Although their city was invaded and burnt to the ground innumerous times by pirates, they always rebuilt it, each time more beautiful than the last. Everyone took part in the profitable smuggling trade – both the common man as well as nobility and clerics.

Around 1750, the sugar trade had already replaced cattle breeding as the most important sector of the economy. 27% of the population were black slaves, who worked the huge plantations surrounding the city. During that time, Spain was not spoken highly of in the elegant salons of Camagüey but it was feared that the Fatherland would give in to the pressure from England and abolish slavery. However: nationalistically motivated resistance against the Spanish existed as well. Among the nationalists were Enrique Varona and later on Ignacio Agramento, a general from the first war of independence. Nicolás Guillén, Cuba's national poet was born in Camagüey. During the 1940s and 1950s, there were several uprisings against the Batista dictatorship. In September 1958, rebel troops lead by "Che" Guevara and Camilo Cienfuegos conquered the city.

Camagüey / **Sights**

There are no really outstanding sights in Camagüey. However, this does not distract from the charm of this city – on the contrary a stroll through the old city districts which are classified as an historical monument is highly recommended, especially after 5 pm when the residents return home from work. Sights one should definitely visit include:

Museo – Casa Natal de Ignacio Agramonte, Calle Agramonte y Candeleria, Plaza de los Trabajadores: the lawyer born in this house in 1841 along with General *Ignacio Agramonte* played a decisive role in composing Cuba's first constitution. In 1873, he fell in the battle of Jimaguaya. The museum displays personal documents from his life.

Iglesia Nuestra Señora de la Merced: The beautiful Nuestra Señora de la Merced church is situated directly across from the Agramonte Casa and houses a magnificent high altar embellished with silver inside.

Teátro Principal: Two blocks from Plaza de los Trabajadores. This theatre is very much worth seeing for its beautiful façade with rounded arches and stained glass windows. The building was restored in the architectural style of the 19th century.

Casa Natal de Nicolás Guillén, Calle Principe, near the Palace of Justice: Guillén is one of the most famous poets in Latin America, he received the Lenin Peace Prize and has acted as chairman of the Cuban Authors Association since 1961. His volume of poetry entitled "Tengo" (I have) from 1967 has been translated into a number of languages. In it, he describes the achievements of the revolution in simple words.

Parque Agramonte: Accessible from Plaza de los Trabajadores via Calle Independencia. Worth seeing in this park is the clay vessel set up there which is almost six feet tall. In earlier times, vessels of this type called "tinajones" were the city's trademark. Spanish seamen first used these vessels for water and oils. Later, they were produced by Catalonian immigrants using the red clay from the Sierra de Cubitas region. Many households use "tinajones" as reservoirs for rainwater.

Also located here in the park is another central library building, the local cultural centre *(Casa de la Trove)* and the cathedral with its beautiful inner nave.

Camagüey / **Practical Information**
Accommodation

Hotel Camagüey, Carretera Central in the eastern portion of the city, Tel: 6218-6805. Double rooms from $29 (£17). Restaurant, bar, cafeteria and swimming pool.

Gran Hotel, Calle Maceo No. 67. Double rooms from $26 (£15.50). This hotel has a type of run-down charm, but also includes a very good restaurant and an entertaining cabaret.

Puerto Principe, Avenida de los Mártires in the northern portion of the city near the train station. Double rooms from $26 (£15.50).

Isla de Cuba, Calle Oscar Primelles; Double rooms from $15 (£9). Simple accommodation near the theatre.

Car Rental

havanautos has an office in Hotel *Camagüey,* Tel: 532-6218.

Excursions

Camagüey lies in a very attractive region in terms of its landscapes. Consequently, the following excursions are recommended:

1. Nuevitas including *Cayo Sabinal.* Nuevitas was the first place that was settled before the advantages and better standard of living was discovered and the town was moved to the site where Camagüey is located today. Nuevitas lies around 75 kilometres (47 miles) to the northeast on the Atlantic coastline. Peace and quiet pervaded for around four hundred years. It was first during the revolution that the town experienced a frantic development. During the 1960s, a large sugar exporting harbour was built and cement and fertiliser factories sprang up. in addition there is a thermoelectric generator station located here.

Nuevitas lies on a bay, the access to the bay being a narrow, natural canal. Situated to the northwest of this canal is the *Cayo Sabinal* peninsula with its long, white beach measuring 16 kilometres (10 miles) in length. Quite often, huge flocks of flamingos can be seen here. The beach of →*Santa Lucia* is located to the southwest, a beach with sugar-white sand with which Cayo Sabinal competes for visitors.

2. Minas. Halfway to Nuevitas is the only place where violins are manufactured in Cuba. This workshop was founded in 1976 by the Ministry of Culture and has been operated by this ministry since then. In addition to violins, guitars are also produced here. Those Cubans obsessed with music hope to break the dependence on imported musical instruments someday.

3. Cangilones del Río Máximo: The Cangilones are limestone cliffs up to 150 metres (490 feet) high and located in the Sierra de Cubitas around 60 kilometres (38 miles) north of Camagüey. The river could erode itself deep into the soft stone, leaving behind round natural pools offering the perfect opportunity to take a dip. The Cangilones are a popular destination for the residents of Camagüey. The best point of departure to explore this region is the small town of *Solá*. Buses depart to Solá daily from the "Terminal de Omnibus Municipales" in Camagüey.

Restaurants

All hotels mentioned above *(→Accommodation, this heading)* have good restaurants. In addition, the following serve excellent food:

La Volante, at Parque Agramonte. Cuban cuisine.

Rancho Luna, Calle Hermanos Agüero. Cuban and international cuisine.

Inexpensive cafeterias and pizzerias can be found on Calle Republica and next to the *Gran Hotel* on Calle Maceo.

Special Events

Camagüey always has a full calendar of events. The best way to obtain information on what is currently happening in Camagüey is to check with the tourist information office in the *Camagüey* Hotel or with the Intur office next to the *Gran Hotel.*

Highlights of the city's cultural scene are the ballet and the symphony orchestra. The folk ensemble "El Grupo de Caidije" is known throughout all of Cuba. Members of this group dance, performing daring leaps and using burning candles and whirling machetes, reminiscent of slavery in Cuba and the neighbouring country of Haiti.

Transportation

Buses: The "Terminal de Omnibus Intermunicipales" lies outside the city on Carretera Central. From here, buses depart for Havana and Santiago de Cuba. The municipal bus line number 10 goes to the old city districts, to the "Terminal de Omnibus Municipales" on Avenida Carlos J. Finlay on the other side of the city. Buses depart from here for Santa Cruz del Sur and Santa Lucia on the northern coast.

Taxis, Collective Taxis: "Piqueras" can be found on the squares in front of the bus terminals.
Trains: The "Estación de Ferrocariles" is located across from the "Terminal de Omnibus Intermunicipales". From here, there is also a train to the small fishing village of Santa Cruz del Sur.

Car Rental

There is every type of make and model of rental cars available to the tourist in Cuba.
Exploring the island by rental car is also an option. Since Spring of 1987, it is also possible to rent a car in *Havana* and give it back in →*Santiago de Cuba.* However, the surcharges for this are considerable and such a tour is only worth the price if the expenses are shared among a number of people.
The state operated car rental agency is called *havanautos* and has the following models available:

Model	1 Day	1 Week	Insurance	Deposit
Fiat Uno	$35 (£21)	$216 (£126)	$8 (£5)	$100 (£58)
Buggy	$35 (£21)	$216 (£126)	$8 (£5)	$100 (£58)
Suzuki Jeep	$40 (£24)	$246 (£143)	$10 (£6)	$100 (£58)
Nissan B-11	$45 (£26)	$277 (£161)	$8 (£5)	$100 (£58)
Nissan Hikari	$80 (£47)	$492 (£286)	$15 (£9)	$300 (£175)
Nissan Vanette	$100 (£58)	$615 (£358)	$10 (£6)	$200 (£120)
Mercedes 190	$130 (£76)	$800 (£466)	$15 (£9)	$1000 (£585)

In addition to the rental price, one must also pay for mileage and fuel. When signing the rental contract, one will receive fuel coupons. The coupons one does not need may be exchanged back. Without the fuel coupons, one will get no fuel. Payment must be made in advance in US dollars. The price includes the first 100 kilometres (63 miles). To rent a car, one must have a valid driving licence and be at least 21 years of age.
It is recommended to reserve a vehicle in advance since availability is limited. Inexpensive cars (VW beetle $35/£21 per day and 20¢/12p per kilometre) are available at "Marazul" in Santa Maria/Playa del Este. *Havanautos* branch offices are located in:
Havana: Agencia Aeropuerto "José Martí", Tel: 5-6 83-30 07 or 30 52;
Agencia Hotel Capri, Tel: 32-64 84 or 32-05 11;
Agencia Hotel Riviera, Tel: 30-50 51;
Playas del Este: Hotel Marazul, Tel: 5-6 87-30 39;
Varadero: Oficina Central, Avenida I y Calle 55, No. 5502, Tel: 5-56-37 33;

Cienfuegos: Hotel Rancho Luna, Tel: 5-4 34-81 20;
Camagüey: Hotel Camagüey, Tel: 5-3 22-7-24 28;
Holguín: Motel El Bosque, Tel: 5-24 48-10 12;
Pinar del Río: Camping Aguas Claras, Tel: 5-8-27 22;
Santiago de Cuba: Motel Leningrado, Tel: 5-22 64-22 21.
The tourist hotels along the beaches rent out bicycles, mopeds, surfboards
and rowboats.

Cardenas

Shortly after Cardenas was founded on March 8, 1828, the city quickly
developed into a bustling centre for trade and commerce. Today, the 70,000
residents live predominantly from the sugar and fish processing industries.
For holiday visitors coming from Varadero only 18 kilometres (11 miles) away,
Carderas offers a good opportunity to experience everyday life in Cuba. The
horse-drawn carriages and the uncompromised perpendicular layout of the
streets themselves characterise the profile of this city.

Cardenas / **Cultural Events**

Every year during the first week of May, a culture week takes place, including
concerts and theatre performances; Carnival is celebrated during November.

Cardenas / **Sights**

Parque Colón: The Parque Colón is the shady focal point of the city and also
the point of departure for a ride in one of the horse-drawn carriages. "La
Dominica" is within sight, formerly the end of a canal leading out to the sea.
Sugar was loaded at this point and later, a hotel was built on this site. In 1919,
the dilapidated *Hotel Donica* building was renovated. The revolutionary government declared it a national monument since the Cuban national flag was
flown here for the first time.

Museo Casa Natal de José Antonio Echeverria, Calle Genes 240; this
building, built in 1873 in the neoclassicistic architectural style, is the house
where the student leader Echeverría was born. He was murdered at the age
of 25 by Batista agents. On display inside are personal articles and photos.

Cayo Largo

The majority of the photos for Cuban tourism brochures are taken on the
paradisical island of Cayo Largo. Lens filters are not necessary, as one will
note when arriving on the island. This island measuring only 3 kilometres (2
miles) in width and 25 kilometres (16 miles) in length has beaches with snow
white sand and the water is crystal clear. Cayo Largo's only reason for
existence seems to be to offer stressed holiday makers peace and relaxation.

There is a runway and a tourist centre on the island as well as numerous idyllic beach bars nestled under palm roofs, where the days seem to fly by while sipping on rum cocktail. The tourist offices in all of the larger hotels organise excursions to Cayo Largo lasting several days.

Cayo Levisa →*Pinar del Río*
Cayo Sabinal →*Camagüey*

Ciego de Avila

Every bus tour leads through the city of Ciego de Avila. Other than this fact the city is of little interest to tourists. The population of 79,000 lives mainly from the dairy industry, but sugar cane and citrus fruits are also harvested here. This city, the capital of the province today, was founded in 1849. There are still some beautiful patrician houses from the 19th century which line the Parque Martí. It is 460 kilometres (288 miles) to →*Havana* and 108 kilometres (68 miles) to →*Camagüey*.

Cienfuegos

Cienfuegos, "linda ciudad del mar" the beautiful city on the sea, was officially founded in 1819. However, Spanish colonists had already settled here at the beginning of the 16th century *(→Cienfuegos/History)* since the location on the protected bay was as ideal as it could get. Today, Cienfuegos has a population of 102,000 and is a busy industrial and commercial city. There is a fishery school and a fishing fleet in the harbour, specially equipped for prawn fishing as well as a large cement factory. The nearby nuclear power plant (the beginning of operations is continually postponed) is the first in Cuba. It is 337 kilometres (211 miles) to Havana. Cienfuegos is the capital of the Cienfuegos province.

Cienfuegos / **History**

In 1514, the first Spanish settlers arrived in this region. The Indian ally Bartolomé de Las Casas, who established an estate here, was also among them. Villages were built all around the bay, without resulting in the founding of the city. This was due to the constant pirate attacks; the pirates often dropped anchor in the bay to supplement their supplies, or rather pillage them. The situation was only to change when the English conquered Jamaica in the 18th century and then greedily set their sights on Cuba. In order to protect the bay which was excellently suited for trade and commerce, the massive *Castillo de Nuestra Señora de los Angeles,* now *Jaguafort* was built on the western shores of the narrow entrance to the bay. The expansion of the bay would follow in 1804. Finally, in 1817, a French emigrant from Louisiana presented the Spanish governor with a plan to settle this area; a plan to which the governor immediately agreed. Two years later land was given to the first settlers, most of whom were French. The city was given the name of the Governor in office at that time, José Cienfuegos. The decades to follow brought a rapid development. Even the devastating cyclones of 1825 and 1888 could not even slow the growth of this city. In addition, Cienfuegos profited from the concurrent fall of the affluent city of → *Trinidad* and after only a short period of time, the young city had taken over Trinidad's role as a commercial hub for the sugar, tobacco and fruit trade. Even today, the city centre provides a good impression of the city's affluence during that time. The wealthy bourgeois families had pompous palaces built and imported all of the necessary items from forks to napkins to silk handkerchiefs from Europe – everything necessary for the elegant "savoir vivre". The slaves, whose work enabled this lavish lifestyle, were kept together among themselves, far from any luxury. And they remained second-class citizens even after slavery was abolished *(→History)*. An apartheid policy was still in existence well into the 1950s.

Cienfuegos / **Sights**

Castillo de Jagua: The Jagua Fortress was built in 1740 and is situated outside the city on the narrow entrance to the bay. At the base of this massive fortress complex lies the small village of Perché. It was founded during the last century by fishermen from Mallorca and Valencia. Many of the residents now secure their livelihood by working in the new *Pasacaballo* Hotel on the opposite side of the bay.

Catedral de Cienfuegos: This church dates back to the early 19th century; it was consecrated on December 7, 1867. Noteworthy inside are the twelve huge windows, an allusion to the twelve apostles.

Parque Martí: Parque Martí is a quiet, green oasis right in the middle of the bustling city. As is often the case in Cuba, live music, is an integral part of this area, taking place almost every evening.

Museo Histórico: The Historical Museum is situated at Parque Martí to the right of the cathedral. On display here are personal articles and weapons belonging to famous patriots from Cienfuegos as well as their photographs.

Casa de Cultura: The House of Culture lies directly across from the cathedral. Concerts and poetry readings often take place here. The programme for special events in Cienfuegos is also available here.

Teátro Tomás Terry: The most beautiful building on Parque Martí is the Teátro Tomás. Caruso performed here as did Sarah Bernhardt and the Bolshoi Ballet. This theatre seats 900. The balconies and boxes inside were built from the most valuable Cuban woods. The theatre was officially opened in 1985 with a performance of the opera "Aida".

Casa de Gobierno (City Hall): The city hall was built after the capitol building in Havana and is now the seat of the "Poder Popular" (→*Politics and Government*).

Museo Naval Nacional, Calle 21, entre Calle 60 y 62: The Naval Museum commemorates September 5, 1957. This was the day on which the marines at the Cienfuegos naval base revolted and fought together with students and members of the M 26 (the July 26th movement) for control over the city. After only a few hours, the uprising was quashed under gunfire from the Batista soldiers.

Palacio de Valle: The Palacio de Valle stands out through its tasteless grotesqueness. It is situated on the Punta Gorda peninsula and was built by a Spanish businessman at the beginning of this century. Later, one of the brothers of the dictator Batista transformed the palace into a casino. The Cuban revolution first used this building as a music academy; meanwhile it serves as an elegant restaurant.

Galeria de Arte, Calle 54, entre 33 y 35: The gallery is situated next to the *La Verja* Restaurant. Works by local artists are on display here.

Cienfuegos / **Practical Information**
Accommodation
Hotel reservations can be made in the "Reservaciones Campismo" office at Calle 31, entre 56 y 58.
Hotels:
Hotel *Jagua,* at the end of Prado (Calle 37) on the Punta Gorda peninsula. A modern tourist hotel with double rooms priced from \$45 (£27). The hotel is accessible by bus numbers 1 and 3 along the Prado.

Hotel *Pasacaballo,* outside of town at the entrance to the bay. A modern tourist hotel with double rooms priced from \$29 (£17). The hotel can be reached inexpensively by motorboat from the "Terminal de Barcos" at the harbour.

Hotel *Rancho Luna,* 15 kilometres (9 miles) outside of the city on the Rancho Luna Beach. A modern hotel complex with buses departing to Cienfuegos five times daily. Double rooms are priced from \$26 (£16).

Hotel *Ciervo de Oro,* Calle 29, entre 56 y 58, offers simple rooms priced around 7 Pesos, often completely booked. Cuban's are preferred as guests.

Hotel *San Carlos,* Calle 50, entre 33 y 35. Simple rooms within the neoclassicistic façade. Rooms are priced from 10 Pesos.

Camping: There are camping areas on Río Caonao near the village of San Fernando de Camarones as well as on Playa El Inglés (the bus to → *Trinidad* passes by there).

Car Rental

The state operated car rental agency *havanautos* runs an office in the Hotel *Rancho Luna*, Tel: 5-432-724 or -8936.

Excursions

Industrial Area: The tourist information offices in the hotels and Cubatur organise tours of the industrial area of Cienfuegos. Things that can be seen here include an oil refinery, grain mills, a cement plant, the first nuclear power plant in Cuba and the largest fully automated sugar loading station in Latin America.

Jardín Botánico (Botanical Gardens): These beautiful gardens are located 25 kilometres (16 miles) outside of Cienfuegos and were laid out by a wealthy American. Later they became a heavily frequented place of study for American students who took part in experiments involving sugar cane. Since the revolution, the Cuban Academy of Science has run the botanical gardens.

One of the two hundred or so beaches lining Cuba's Caribbean coast

Meanwhile. over 2,000 species of plants, 20 types of bamboo and numerous exotic trees can be found on these grounds.

Playa Rancho Luna: The Rancho Luna Beach lies in the eastern districts of the city near the Rancho Luna Hotel. This is a narrow, sand beach but does make a nice diving area. Buses depart for this beach five times daily from the bus terminal.

Restaurants

Mandarin, Paseo del Prado, serving Chinese specialities.

1819, Paseo del Prado, Creole cuisine in a colonial atmosphere.

El Pollito, Paseo del Prado, chicken prepared in a number of ways.

La Verja, Avenida 54 No. 3306, serving Creole and international cuisine. The "noche cubana" takes place every Saturday.

El Polinesio, at Parque Martí, serving Creole and Polynesian dishes.

El Cochinito, Avenida 37 No. 5612, at the end of the Prado; serving delicious pork dishes.

Covadonga, at the end of the Prado before Hotel *Jagua*. Spanish cuisine.

La Laguna, Avenida 10, esq. a 47, serving fish and mussel dishes.

All of the restaurants open at lunchtime and close around 11 pm. The prices range from 10 to 15 pesos. In addition there are numerous inexpensive cafeterias and pizzerias. One nice place is *Pizzeria Air Libre,* Calle 56, entre Calle 29 y 31. Here, one can dine outdoors under a pergola.

Tourist Information

Cubatur, Calle 56.

Transportation

Bus: There is only one bus station in Cienfuegos. This station offers services to nearby areas and faraway cities. The bus station is located on Calle 56 esq. a 49. Only one bus departs daily to Havana, therefore it is recommended to first go to →*Santa Clara* unless one has made a seat reservation six days in advance at the "Reservaciones Omnibus Nacional" office at Calle 54 entre 35 y 37. Recently, a system has been introduced where tickets are purchased in advance and then validated in the bus. Tickets for 10 Centavos are available at the ticket office near the bus stop at Calle 37 as well as at news stands.

Taxi: There is a taxi stand in front of the bus station.

Trains: The train station is located at Calle 58, esq. a 49. The train to →*Havana* departs daily.

Climate

Cuba lies in a zone bordering the tropics. Its central and western regions experience a dry season lasting three to five months during the winter,

	Havana	Cienfuegos	Camajuani	Camagüey
Average Air	75 m/245ft	39 m/128ft	100 m/327ft	118 m/ 386ft
Temperature °C(°F)				
Coldest Month (January)	21.7 (71.1)	22.2 (72.0)	19.7 (67.5)	22.0 (71.6)
Warmest Month (August)	27.2 (81.0)	27.2 (81.0)	25.4 (77.7)	27.6 (81.7)
Annual Monthly Average	24.6 (76.3)	25.0 (77.0)	22.9 (73.2)	25.1 (77.2)
Average Daily High °C(°F)				
Coldest Month (December)	26.3 (79.3)	27.2 (81.0)	–	28.5 (83.3)
Warmest Month (August)	31.5 (88.7)	32.2 (90.0)	–	33.7 (92.7)
Average High	28.8 (83.8)	30.0 (86.0)	–	31.2 (88.2)

approximately between November and March. This is the best time for touring the island.

Typical of Cuban summers are short but heavy rainstorms. A constantly humid, tropical rainy climate dominates the southeastern regions of the island with 1,500 mm (58 inches) of precipitation annually.

Clothing and Equipment

It is difficult to replace loss or damage to electrical or photographic goods in Cuba. Thus the selection in the Intur Shops in the tourist hotels is lacking and overpriced while the shops on the free market offer goods produced in the former Eastern block with a different standard.

Humidity is high. Synthetic materials are better left at home; one should definitely bring along cotton clothing. What of course is necessary is swimwear since Cuba has over 200 beaches. For visiting better restaurants and night-clubs, it is recommended to wear trousers and long sleeve shirts for men and also this type of attire for women. Most restaurants are equipped with air conditioning which works so well one might need a warm sweater. The following articles are difficult to find in Cuba: cosmetics, deodorant and shampoo, insect repellent, laundry detergent, glue stick for stamps, writing materials, airmail envelopes, ballpoint pens, bottle openers, film, sunglasses and hats, adapters for shavers, batteries.

Credit Cards →*Currency Regulations and Exchange*
Documents →*Travel Documents*

Cojimar

The small fishing village of Cojimar was founded in 1646 and gained world literary fame 300 years later through the Nobel prize-winning narration "The Old Man and the Sea" by Ernest Hemingway. The American author was very well liked in this town and the residents have erected a memorial to "their" Hemmingway across from the fortress on the coast. The fishermen's pub "La

Hemmingway across from the fortress on the coast. The fishermen's pub "La Terreza", in which the boy goes to fetch the exhausted Santiago a cup of hot coffee in the story, is still in existence and still serves delicious fish dishes in a pleasant atmosphere. The specialities are mussels and lobster. The fishing pub "La Terraza" is open from 6 pm daily.

Today Cojimar is on the outskirts of Havana and can be reached by taxi or bus number 58, at the Calle 58, the Capitol stop.

Crime

Travelling in Cuba is safer than in any other Latin American country. The revolution provided every Cuban with a modest affluence; however, the penalties for theft are also extreme. In the beach areas and tourist centres, one should still keep an eye on one's belongings. Typically western articles of clothing like T-shirts and jeans are preferred items in Cuba. In hotel rooms, some items like shampoo or shaving lotion have been known to disappear if they have not been put away.

Cubatur → *Travelling in Cuba / Cubatur*

Cuisine

All tourist hotels have at least one restaurant serving international and Cuban cuisine. In recent times an increasing number of hotels has started offering their guests buffets. People who are not hotel guests are of course also welcome. On entering the hotel restaurants, the hotel card must be presented when checking in at the desk. The payment is expected in hard currency, usually in US dollars. Many hotel restaurants also have "noche cubana" once a week. This is when typical Cuban cuisine is served.

A breakfast consisting of a cup of coffee, bread, butter, an egg, jam and fruit juice costs around \$2.50/£1.45. Both lunch and dinner are priced around \$8/£4.65.

Tourists should definitely make reservations when visiting one of the top restaurants not housed in the hotels. If one's ability to speak the Spanish language is sufficient then this can be done by telephone, otherwise the reception or the Cubatur offices in the hotels will do it. (→ *Travelling in Cuba/Cubatur and Intur*).

In the restaurants in Havana and Varadero, payment in US dollars is expected. In the other cities you usually pay in Cuban pesos. Two pesos will be enough

White castlines, lush vegetation and water with a constant temperature of around 25 °C (77 °F): attributes that would please any tourism manager

pizzerias or cafés. The quickest service is always at the bar where one should definitely ask which service is provided and who is responsible for which area of the bar to order even though there are more service personnel behind the counter than there are guests in front of it. One is seated at a table by the "capitán" or the "capitana". Seats near the powerful air conditioning should be immediately rejected since they can get unpleasantly chilly after only an hour. And another thing: for the guests at one table only one bill is made out. Asking for separate bills always seems to cause undreamt of problems having to do with lacking Spanish skills. It is better to discuss who will pay before entering the restaurant and settle the bill later.

Those who forego reserving a table are well advised to show up early at a restaurant. Lunch is served around noon and dinner around 7 pm. Later restaurants tend to run out of certain dishes especially vegetables and fruit juices.

"Cocina Criolla" – Cuban Cuisine

The traditional Cuban dishes are very sweet and anything but light – Cubans enjoy eating and eating large portions.

The following **specialities** can be found both on the tables in Cuban homes as well as on the menus in restaurants.

"Moros y christianos": the "walls and Christians" made from rice and beans is Cuba's national dish.

"Arroz congris": Rice with red beans originating from the Oriente region. The term "congris" comes from "riz á la Conjo" (rice á la Congo) and was brought over from the French coffee plantations on Haiti.

"Tamales": corn tortillas filled with meat and spices.

"Malanga": oblong bland tasting roots which are rich in starch and were already grown by the native Indian population. Before the revolution this was the main food staple for the poorer population.

"Yuca": a tuber of light stringy texture. Extremely rich in starch, also called "maniok" or "cassava".

"Platano verde": Cooking bananas or plantanes, popular as a side dish.

"Fufu": Mixed cooking bananas with roasted, crumbled pork rind. This comes from Africa and is especially popular in Santiago de Cuba among other cities.

Meat, in contrast to earlier times, is meanwhile available to everyone. Since the revolution, meat consumption has increased drastically.

"carne de res": beef.

"carne de puerco" or "cerdo": pork, very tasty and very juicy.

"conejo": rabbit, a Cuban speciality.

"pollo": chicken.

Fish is still difficult to find considering that Cubans have adapted their eating customs to meat. Fish dishes are almost exclusively offered only in the tourist hotels. Side dishes are usually rice, yuca or malanga. Vegetables are scarce; therefore, tomato salads are usually quite paltry.

The most popular **desserts** include creme caramel "natilla" (vanilla pudding) or ice cream. Cuban ice cream is very good, evidence of the productivity of Cuba's dairy industry. Ice cream parlours, called "coppelias", can be found in almost every larger town.

"helado": a large scoop of ice cream.

"jimaguas": two large scoops.

"ensalada": several smaller scoops of ice cream.

"sundae": ice cream served with fruit.

"lolita": ice cream with pudding.

An extra portion is called "addicional".

Café Cubano, Rum and More

Cubans drink their **coffee** where other nations drink beer: at the bar. Countless coffee "pubs" are heavily frequented late into the night by Cuban guests, enjoying their "café cubano". This brew is drunk black, hot and sweet. In addition, there is also "café mesclado". It contains a 20% proportion of other roasted products. "Café américano" is most similar to "normal" coffee with cream; "café con leche" is a mixture of around 1 part strong coffee and 3 parts steamed milk.

Despite all of this, the most famous Cuban drink was and remains **rum.** It emerged as a byproduct from the production of sugar and was the favourite drink of seamen between Cape Horn and the Bearing Strait up to the 18th century. Later, the distilling process was developed that made the Cuban rum into the best in the world. Large distilleries sprang up like weeds and the Bacardi family became the leader in rum production.

When the North Americans got the idea to use rum as a base for cocktails and mixed drinks, Cuba had problems keeping up with the demand. After the victory of the revolution, the rum producers quickly fled the island. The Bacardi's had their name registered as a trademark and took this asset with them to Puerto Rico to supply the rum-lovers of the world.

Despite the difficulties with the loss of specialised workers and service personnel, Cuba managed to uphold the rum tradition. The new product is called "Habana Club" and in terms of quality, it is just as good as Bacardi. There are three classes of quality: "Carta Blanca" – "ligero y seco" (light and dry); "Carta de Oro" – "dorado y seco" (golden-yellow and dry); "Añejo" – brown rum, aged up to seven years. For cocktails, the lighter rum is used. A good bar tender will have memorised several hundred cocktails. The most popular **drinks** include:

"Daiquiri": a delicious alcoholic, blended ice cocktail... ingredients: rum, lime juice, sugar, a few squirts of bitters and crushed ice, mixed in a blender.

"Mojito": along with the "Daiquiri", this is one of the most renowned among Cuban cocktails and a favourite of the prominent drinker Ernest Hemingway (→*Cojimar*). Ingredients: rum, a mint sprig, lemon juice, soda water and lots of ice.

"Cuba Libre": Rum filled to the top of the glass with ice cubes and topped off with Tropicola (Cuban cola substitute). "Ron Collins": Rum, sugar, lime juice, ice and soda water.

"Planters Punch": rum, sugar, pineapple, cherries, oranges, some soda water and ice.

"Mary Pickford": pineapple juice, rum, ice and some grenadine.

"Mulata": a dark "Daiquiri". Rum lime, some cocoa liqueur, blended with ice.

"Presidente": Rum, vermouth and grenadine.

While the tourist can't seem to get enough of the cocktails and mixed drinks, beer is the most popular drink among the Cubans. The most widely sold types of beer are "cerveza clara", a light and pleasant beer, and "Hatuey", a strong beer with the profile of the famous Cuban Indian chief on the label.

The best place to sample a daiquiri — one of Hemingway's favourites — is at the "Floridita" bar in Havana

Wine is horrendously expensive since it is imported from Eastern European countries

Cultural Institutions

The core of Cuban cultural policy is: Art should educate the people; Cuban culture should evolve into folk culture through everyone's active participation. After the revolution, numerous cultural facilities were founded like the National Art Academy of Havana, the Authors and Artists' Association, the "casa de las américas" (responsible for cultural exchange in Latin America) and the governments publishing house. The "casas de la cultura" have been in existence since 1977. They are similar to community colleges and are spread all across Cuba. Books are very inexpensive since no demands are placed on the quality of paper or the outer appearance. World literature is printed as Cuba sees fit since the country resigned membership from the Copyright Conventon in 1967. Those looking to be active in the literary field will find the literary workshops an excellent opportunity — these have been in existence since the 1960s.

Currency

The currency of Cuba is the peso Cubano. Bank notes in circulations are in the denominations of 1,3,5,10 and 20 pesos as well as coins of 1,5,10 and 20 centavos. Tourists usually find the bright red three-peso notes especially appropriate as a souvenir with the portrait of "Che" Guevara in his famous revolutionary pose. However, one should not forget that taking Cuban currency out of the country is strictly prohibited.

Currency Exchange and Regulations

Foreign currency may be brought into the country in unlimited amounts. Each tourist must declare the currencies in his prosession. This declaration is then handed over when entering the country. When exchanging money into Cuban pesos, one will be given a receipt since it is necessary to have this when leaving the country in order to be able to exchange any unspent pesos back.The amount one can exchange back is, however, limited to 50 Cuban pesos. Currency is exchanged in every hotel, branches of the Banco Nacional and in the tourism centres. Note: the currency used at the tourism centres is the US dollars. Counters in the hotels and even in the Banco Nacional often don't have sufficient supplies in the foreign currencies. It is therefore, recommended to exchange money when the opportunity presents itself. As long as they are not issued by a US bank, all of the standard travellers cheques are accepted. Eurocheques, however, are not accepted.

Visitors in the tourism centres will hardly come into contact with the national currency. Hotels, nightclubs, restaurants, excursions and flights as well as shopping in the state-run Intur shops in the hotels only accept hard foreign currency. Since individual tourists quite often take advantage of the tourist infrastructure, they should have travellers cheques made out in US dollars and bring along some cash as well.

One can indeed also pay in Cuban pesos in the tourist centres; however, these are only accepted with the presentation of a currency exchange receipt. In general, this is not common practice. To the confusion of the visitor, there is also a type of tourist currency. The coins, along with the US coins serve as change and the bank notes ("certificados") can be received at the bank instead of dollars. At tourist centres these are just as acceptable as US dollars, but outside these areas, in the Cuban everyday, they are not worth the paper they are printed on. Another reason to exchange currencies into US dollars when the opportunity presents itself. Dollars are namely more flexible and must not be exchanged back when leaving the country.

A few words on the black currency market: buying, selling, exchange or transfer of foreign currencies to Cuban nationals is prohibited. The black market flourishes despite this, not lastly due to individual travellers needing pesos whilst travelling away from the normal tourist centres. Especially in Havana, Varadero and Santiago de Cuba *(→individual entries)* tourists are often approached by young people, saying "cambio". In 1992 the black market exchange rate peaked at 1 to 20. For the individual traveller certainly enticing; budgeting becomes a thing of the past. However: in order to actually *use* this exchanged money in Havana and Varadero, one must have excellent to near perfect Spanish skills and present a convincing imitation of a Cuban or a specialised worker from one of the allied socialist countries. Tourists are not seriously prosecuted for exchanging money on the black market; however Cubans citizens do get into quite a lot of trouble if they are caught. When the day is over, black market currency exchange does involve a personal risk. Among those exchanging on the black market are also shady characters who do not hesitate to use force to get what they want. To later report this to the police is indeed a tedious process as one could expect.

Customs Regulations

All items for personal use may be brought into Cuba in addition to two bottles of alcoholic beverages and one carton of cigarettes. Items which must be declared include: cameras, transistor radios, portable typewriters, sports and fishing equipment, firearms for hunting and jewellery. When leaving the country, any items declared must also be taken back out. The entry declaration should be kept for possible spot checks upon departure. Drugs and pornographic materials are, of course, not allowed to be brought into Cuba. This is also true for weapons, explosives and games of chance. Animal and plant products will also be confiscated.

When leaving the country, one may take along: 50 cigars, 200 cigarettes, 1 litre of alcoholic beverages, 250 grams of coffee and any handicrafts.

Driving Licence →*Travel Documents*

Economy

Economy / **General Development since 1959**

The two agricultural reforms of 1959 and 1963 radically changed the ownership of land and were intended to jolt production out of its one-sided one crop economy. Still many small-scale, private farmers did remain. Their children began to take advantage of the educational opportunities created by the revolution and learn trades and professions which had nothing more to do with agriculture. The result was a migration to the cities. In order to keep young people in rural areas, production cooperatives were established in 1977. In joining such a cooperative, the farmer not only has access to specialised consultation but also enjoys social improvements like a sturdy house, running water, a refrigerator and electricity. The association into cooperatives is voluntary. The success of this programme: migration out of rural areas is unknown in Cuba.

The decentralisation of the administrative structures has resulted in a noticeable improvement in the economy. Material motivation instead of appeals to the revolutionary consciousness serve to increase productivity today. In the factories, the system of economic accounting has been introduced, whereby production is geared to profit and profitability.

The picture is much more bleak on the international scene. The "terms of trade" are miserable. Prices for imports are constantly on the rise, while less and less can be bought with the income generated by exports. Cuba is in debt to foreign countries to the tune of 3,000,000,000 US dollars and even had to refinance this debt through the World Bank in 1985. With the political changes in east bloc nations in 1989, Cuba was forced more and more into the corner. Deliveries to Cuba were cut sharply or discontinued altogether. The economic sanctions from the USA also hit hard.

To what degree these factors are responsible for the situation in Cuba can be seen from the fact that Cuba was almost exclusively dependent on the former USSR and the other east bloc nations. Coupled with this, the rigid planned economy in Cuba stifled any individual initiative. Proposed solutions tend toward having Cuba revert to market economy methods as often as necessary, for example the privatisation of services, restaurants, small merchants etc. What will come of these proposals – and how and if Cuba can free itself from this crisis – remains to be seen.

Economy / **Agriculture**

Even today, sugar remains the focus of the Cuban economy despite all efforts to move away from the monoculture. However, it proved possible to turn this situation to the positive by modernising sugar production through computer technology. A large proportion of revenues flowed into the development of new sectors of production and today, citrus fruits, textiles and the construction industry as well as livestock breeding and nickel mining are of enormous importance to the Cuban economy.

El Cobre

The small settlement of El Cobre was named after a copper mine and lies only a few kilometres from Santiago de Cuba in the Sierra Maestra. The mountain slopes show the traces of the mining work that lasted for over four hundred years and was undertaken at first by the Indians and then by African slaves. Around 1550 the German Welser trading company sent their mining engineer Hans Tetzel to Santiago under the request of the Spanish governor. Tetzel immediately began with the planned exploitation of the rich copper deposits. He also founded the settlement of El Cobre. A hundred years later were the first *Visions of Mary* at the settlement and a church was built in honour of Mary who had meanwhile become the patron saint of the nation. With this, the settlement also became the place of pilgrimage for thousands. The church's revenues increased enormously and thus the cathedral which now stands in this area was built at the end of the 19th century.

Near the entrance are numerous votive offerings such as an offering by the first Cuban cosmonaut which is a glass of soil from his home town as well as Hemingway's Nobel Prize medallion which he received for "The Old Man and The Sea" *(→Cojimar, →Santiago de Cuba/ Excursions).*

Electricity

The electrical current is 110 volts with US standard sockets. Those coming from European countries will need an adaptor.

Visions of the Virgin Mary in El Cobre lead to the construction of this magnificent cathedral, a destination for pilgrims from all over the world

Embassies and Consulates

British Embassy, 8th Floor, Edificio Bolívar, Carcel 101-103 (just off Prado), La Habana, Tel: 71086/7/8.

United States Interests Section, Calzada, Calle L and M, Vedado, Tel: 320551/59 and 329700.

Canadian Embassy, Calle 30, No. 518, La Habana, Miramar, Tel: 26421 and 26422.

Argentinean Embassy, Calle 36, No. 511, La Habana, Miramar, Tel: 225540 and 225549.

Ecuadoran Embassy, 5ta Ave, No. 4407, La Habana, Miramar, Tel: 296839 and 292004.

Embassy of Guyana, Calle 18, No. 506, La Habana, Miramar, Tel: 221249 and 222494.

Mexican Embassy, Calle 12 No. 518La Habana Miramar Tel: 28634 and 28198.

Nicaraguan Embassy, 7ma., Avenida No. 1402, La Habana, Miramar, Tel: 26810 and 26882.

Embassy of Panamá, Calle 26, No. 109, La Habana, Miramar, Tel: 222096 and 221893.

Peruvian Embassy, Calle 36 A, Tel: 222096 and 221893, No. 704, La Habana Miramar, Tel: 294477

Venezuelan Embassy, 5ta Ave, No. 7802, La Habana, Miramar, Tel: 225497 and 221862

Geography

While in exile, the Cuban national poet Nicolás Guillén once compared the shape of his homeland to that of a lizard. And seen on a map the island does actually look so much like a lizard, that the industry took up on this similarity and had thousands of T-shirts printed with a laughing crocodile motif.

Around 110,000 square kilometres (42,900 square miles) in area, Cuba is the largest island in the Antilles. Direct neighbours include Haiti 80 kilometres (50 miles) to the east, Jamaica to the south, Mexico 200 kilometres (125 miles) beyond the westernmost point of Cuba, the Bahamas to the northeast and the United States, separated from Cuba by the Florida strait, 180 kilometres (112.5 miles) wide.

Its strategical location made Cuba a pawn for 450 years for the colonial powers and the USA. The Spaniards used the island as an intermediate station for its legendary Silver Fleet while the United States following on the heels of Spain viewed Cuba as an additional state, despite this they exploited the Cuban economy *(→History)*.

The landscapes of the island are characterised by extensive plains and rolling hills. The highest mountain ranges are the still impenetrable Sierra Maestra with the highest elevation Pico Turquino (1,947 metres/6,366 feet) in the Oriente, the Sierra del Escambray in the southern central regions of the island and the Cordillera de Guaniguanico (652 metres/2,132 feet) in the western most regions of Cuba. While 75% of the island was covered in forests when the Spanish arrived, only the northern slopes of the Sierra Maestra mountain range have some remnants of the lush vegetation. Other forest regions fell victim to the fire clearing for sugar cane or the wood was used for Spanish wharfs and carpentry workshops during colonial times. Since the revolution, extensive reforestation projects have been undertaken to increase the forest areas of Cuba.

The highland plains are unfertile, a habitat for little more than thorny bushes and cactuses. If the soil is slightly richer, then one can find the massive royal palms. This tree is on Cuba's coat of arms and grows up to 40 metres (131 feet) in height, providing farmers with wood; its bark and leaves providing valuable materials for producing furnishings, baskets and thatched roofs.

The coastline almost 6,000 kilometres (3,750 miles) in length is lined with mangrove forests and swamps. The white beaches one will see in tourism brochures account for only a small portion of the coastline. What is much more typical are the rugged, rocky sections of coastline.

In Cuba the rivers are typically shallow and short, the two exceptions being the Río Cujaguateje in the west and the Río Cauto in the Sierra Maestra. The latter being the longest river in Cuba of a length of 370 kilometres (231 miles). In the delta and flood plains of the rivers, rice has increasingly been planted since the revolution.

Most of the rivers dry to a tickle during the dry season. During the rainy season they then swell to rushing currents and flood extensive areas. In order to regulate and to use the large quantities of water, numerous reservoirs have been built since the 1960s. The largest of these are the Presa Zaza near →*Sancti Spiritus* and Hanabanilla near →*Santa Clara.*

Gibara

Gibara is a small fishing town with a population of 58,000 situated on the Atlantic coast. The name of this town is indeed Gibara which comes from the Indian word "jiba", the term for a shrub indigenous to this area; however, most Cubans only know the town as "La Villa Blanca", the white town. Numerous Cubans visit Gibara during weekends to enjoy the pleasant atmosphere of this town. Worth seeing in GIbara is the Museo de Ambiente Cubano del siglo XIX, Calle Independencia No. 27. The museum is housed in the former home of a wealthy family of tobacco merchants, displaying furniture and ceramics from the colonial 19th century in eleven rooms.

Gran Piedra National Park and La Isabelica

Located 32 kilometres (20 miles) northwest of Santiago de Cuba, the Gran Piedra National Park is a popular recreation area used by the residents of Santiago as well as a famous tourist attraction. The road to the park winds over serpentines through the dark pine forests of the mountainous landscape, offering numerous panoramas of the Caribbean Sea. Up on the crest of the mountains, at an elevation of almost 1,000 metres (3,270 feet) lies the *Motel Gran Piedra* (reservations can be made through the Cubatur office in Santiago) with its modernly appointed bungalows. The *Gran Piedra* a massive boulder around 50 metres (164 feet) high and over 60,000 tons towers over everything else. A steep footpath leads up to the boulder. One must climb a ladder up onto the rock itself. From this vantage point, one can see all the way to Jamaica given clear weather. Inland and somewhat below the boulder, the old coffee plantation *La Isabelica* can be seen, one of seven plantations in this region. Today it is a museum open to the public. The footpath leading to the plantation takes around half an hour to traverse. The residential house was built at the beginning of the 19th century by a French farmer. Coffee beans were spread out to dry on the large, level area in front of the house. The bell at the entrance to the residential tract was used to call the slaves to work. A small path leads to a renovated coffee mill in which beans were peeled. The mill was powered by oxen. Also worth visiting are the botanical gardens, located at the beginning of the Gran Piedra incline. The route there is, however, very adventuresome. (→*Santiago de Cuba/Excursions*).

Granjita Siboney

This small farm lies on the coastal road around 13 kilometres (8 miles) east of Santiago de Cuba. Its name is closely connected to the storming of the Moncada base by young rebels in 1953 (→*History*). Over 100 men hid in the four rooms of this farmhouse the night before the attack. Fidél Castro's best friend Abel Santamaría had bought the farm and used it as a chicken farm for cover. Batista's secret service was everywhere after all, and one could not depend on the discretion of the neighbours. Weapons and uniforms were hidden in the well next to the house. The attack on the barracks failed the survivors fled back to the Granjita Siboney farm, government soldiers hot on their heels. A fierce shooting took place before the house, as evidenced by the numerous bullet holes on the façade.

Today the farm is a museum which attracts "revolutionary pilgrims" from around the world. On display in the rooms are uniforms, weapons, newspaper articles and photos which document the planning stages and the course of events. The road to Granjita is lined with memorial markers honouring the rebel fighters (→*Santiago de Cuba Excursions*).

Guamá

Guamá – actually Boca de Guamá – lies on the route to the →*Bay of Pigs* and is a popular stop-over for both domestic and international tourists. It lies on the *Laguna del Tesoro* one of the largest natural lakes in Cuba. According to legend, the Indian Chief Guamá sank the golden treasures belonging to his people in the lake before leading his subjects into the last battle against the Spaniards. Since then, this lake is known as "Treasure Lake". An Indian style stilt village along the shore is reminiscent of these times. The village was laid out in 1960 to spur on the economy in this otherwise neglected region through tourism. At first, the village was predominantly planned for the local residents, who could spend their honeymoon here. Meanwhile, the complex is also open to international tourists. In addition, another entire Indian village was reconstructed nearby according to old documents. It provides an impression of how the native population once lived.

Also nearby is a large *Crocodile Farm* (Centro de recria cocodrilos). Several endangered crocodile species are bred in smaller and larger pools. A further attraction is a trip on the "Treasure Lake" in a boat with a larger keel. Passengers are taken out to the lake through a canal. With a lot of luck, one might see a "manati" an almost extinct species of sea cow.

Caution: Definitely bring along insect repellent; the mosquitoes in Guamá are merciless.

Guamá / **Practical Information**

Accommodation: *Villa Guamá,* Double rooms from $29 (£17). The rooms are equipped with a bathroom, air conditioning, television and telephone. This holiday complex also includes a restaurant, a bar, a cafeteria and a discotheque.

Guanahacabibes

The rocky and barren Guanahacabibes Peninsula lies in the western extremities of Cuba 106 kilometres (66 miles) southwest of Pinar del Río. Its swamps were a last resort for the Indians belonging to the Guanahatabeyes tribe. One of the largest continual forests in Cuba still covers the peninsula. Meanwhile, this area has been declared a national park. Here, one can see deer, wild boars and exotic birds. Buses only operate to La Bajada from there one is dependent on friendly local residents. For buses to La Bajada →*Pinar del Río*.

Guantánamo

It is impossible to speak of Guantánamo without mentioning the US Marine base located there. The city itself has nothing to offer in the way of tourism. With the exception of few beautiful houses built in the Spanish colonial style, there is nothing worth seeing. For those who pass Guantánamo on their way to Baracoa, a few statistics: the city was founded in 1797 and is now home to a population of 165,000. During the 19th century the residents lived from the production of sugar; at that time, black slaves accounted for 44% of the population. The US Marine base was set up shortly after Cuba's independence and despite protest from Havana, has not been dismantled to date.

Guardalavaca

Guardalavaca is a strange name for a beach in a magnificent location. Presumably, the name comes from "guardalabarca", " guard the boat", which evolved into "guardalavaca", "guard the cow" — through linguistic laziness. The first name is not improbable since the coastline with its numerous small bays offered pirates the perfect chance to hide their boats. Sand and vegetation here are just to the liking of the tourist industry: white sand and lush vegetation. The three kilometres (2 mile) beach is framed by rugged cliffs covered in green, making it an oasis of relaxation. The water temperature hovers around a constant 25°C(77°F). Guardalavaca lies around 50 kilometres (31 miles) northeast of Holguín and 186 kilometres (116 miles) north of Santiago de Cuba.

Guardalavaca/ **Practical Information**

Accommodation

Hotel Guardalavaca, directly on the beach, restaurant, cafeteria, bar, discotheque, swimming pool. All rooms with full bath. Double rooms are priced from $30 (£18).

Villa Guardalavaca, a very nice holiday complex with a restaurant, bar and discotheque. All of the bungalows are equipped with a bathroom. Priced from $20 (£12).

Excursions

The tourist office in *Hotel Guardalavaca* organises interesting excursions to the nearby regions. Definitely worth visiting are:

– the *Indocuban Museum* of →*Banes,* 30 minutes from Guardalavaca taking one of the most beautiful roadways in Cuba.

– *Puerto Bariay.* This is where Columbus landed on October 29, 1492.

– *Mayarí.* Archaeologists discovered around one third of pre-Columbian tools in the limestone caverns nearby.

Hanabanilla

Hanabanilla is a reservoir in the Sierra del Escambray located 50 kilometres (31 miles) south of Santa Clara, just as far east of Cienfuegos and around 80 kilometres (50 miles) north of Trinidad. Constructed by the revolutionary government during the 1960s, this reservoir now provides the cities of Santa Clara and Cienfuegos with drinking water. A small hydroelectric plant supplies the nearby areas with electricity. This portion of the Escambray Mountains counts among the most beautiful in all of Cuba. The lush vegetation on the crest of this mountain range are reflected in the smooth surface, of the lake. The lake also offers excellent fishing. The terrace belonging to the *Hotel Hanabanilla* perched above the lake offers a fantastic view of the lake and surrounding areas. All around are the homes of farm workers and tobacco farmers who are brought to work by small ferries. On the opposite shores "hanging" on a mountain slope like a swallow nest is the *Río Negro Restaurant*. Excursions to the reservoir are organised by the tourist offices in Hotels in Havana, Varadero and Cienfuegos (→*individual entries*).

Havana

Havana officially called "Ciudad de la Habana" is Cuba's capital. With a population of over two million, it is also the largest city in Cuba. Predominantly of interest are the districts of *Habana Vieja* (Old Havana), *Centro Habana* (Central Habana), and *Vedado* (this is where most of the hotels are located). One will at most take a stroll through the preferred area *Miramar* where the embassies are situated. One will pass by the outer districts of *La Habana, Guanabacoa* and *Cojimar* on the way to the city's beaches.

Havana/ **History**

The festive founding of the San Cristóbal de la Habana settlement took place on July 25, 1519, supposedly on the site where the Plaza de Armas is located today. Due to its function as intermediate station and gateway to the new world, Havana grew rapidly. Even repeated attacks by internationally active pirates could not hinder this city's development. In 1552, Havana became Cuba's capital. Three years later the infamous French pirate Jacques de Sores plundered the city to such a degree that the Spanish began with the construction of the *La Fuerza* fortress and the twin bastions of El Morro and *La Punta* almost before the sails of the pirate ship had disappeared over the horizon. Havana was awarded the rights of a city in 1592. In 1654, a third of its population fell victim to an epidemic of yellow fever. Despite this, the city was able to achieve prosperity especially due to the profitable slave trade in the New World. Construction on the city wall began in 1674. The residents feared the invasion of the Britons who had conquered Jamaica. Shortly before,

1728 marked the founding of the University. August 13, 1762 was a black day in the city's chronicles: after a two-month occupation, the city ultimately did fall to the Britons. However, after a year they left the island in exchange for Florida. The rubble from the occupation was cleared away and the city was given the appearance it has today.

Famous architects transformed Havana into the most beautiful city in Latin America. The city wall was razed in 1863 to make room for the expansion of the city. The year 1871 would have a terrible event in store: because of criticism aimed at the Spanish colonial rule, and the alleged desecration of a grave where a Spanish journalist was buried, eight medical students were shot to death by a firing squad. 1898 was an historically significant year as well. The explosion of the US cruiser "Maine" in the harbour basin was the motivation for the United States to enter the second Cuban war of independence and influence the outcome to their advantage. Under their political and economic influence, Havana developed into a "fallen" beauty. Hotels, casinos and brothels sprang up like weeds, all under the control of the mafia. A continuous ring of slums quickly enclosed the city. The affluent class lived in the Miramar and Vedado districts, completely isolated from the rest of the city by a security patrol force. At the beginning of 1959, the victorious rebel army led by Fidél Castro and "Che" Guevara marched into Havana after they had achieved the conclusive victory over the dictator Batista's army after battles lasting three years.

Havana / **Sights**

Havana is big and almost unbearable during the midday heat. Those who think they can set off to explore the city on their own despite this, should set a relaxed pace and take their time. One should also have at least a basic command of the Spanish language. Discovering the city on one's own is an especially attractive alternative in Havana. Buses depart for every corner of the city but no one knows where they're coming from or where they're headed (→*Travel in Cuba*). There are of course, also taxis and huge old American cars which roll along the "avenidas", used as collective taxis.

Sightseeing tours – a practical option to supplement a tour of the city – are organised by Cubatur (→*Travel in Cuba*) and can be booked in any of the large hotels.

There are actually two Havanas: *La Habana Vieja* (Old Havana) and *La Habana Moderna* (Modern Havana). Both are worth seeing since they reflect different epochs in Cuba's history.

Sights in Habana Vieja

The largest proportion of tourists arrive in the hotel district of *Vedado*. It is only a four minute walk from here to the old city. (For information on buses and taxis →*Practical Information*).

La Plaza de Armas, Calle Obispo, O'Reilly Tacóu y Baratillo. La Plaza de Armas is the oldest square in Havana. The first Spanish settlement dates back to the 16th century. Due to its proximity to the harbour and Governor's Palace, it formed the focus of social life up to the 19th century.

El Templete, a small temple on the eastern side of the square was built in honour of the city's founding fathers. Erected in 1828, it stands exactly on the site where the mass in honour of the city's founding was held on July 25, 1519. Directly adjacent to the right of the temple is the *Palacio del Conde de Santovenia* (Palace of the Count of Santovenia). It originates from the second half of the 18th century. Later a wealthy American transformed this building into a hotel named "Santa Isabel". Today there is a restaurant on the ground floor, *Meson de la Flota de Habana.*

Across from *El Templete,* one will see the *Palacio de los Capitanes Generales* (Palace of the Governor General). This building erected in the late Baroque architectural style dates back to 1776 and served as the seat of the highest governmental authorities in Cuba up to 1898. After that, the Palace was occasionally used by the US interventionary government on occasion. From 1920 to 1958, it served as the city hall and then as the revolutionary municipal administration building up to 1968. Since then, it has housed the Municipal Museum. The bells at the entrance originate from watch towers for the large plantations. A statue of Christopher Columbus stands in the inner courtyard. The north side of Plaza de Armas is bordered by the *Palacio del Segundo Cabo*. It was built in 1772 for the Spanish Military Commissariat. Today it houses the Ministry of Culture.

At the centre of the square is a monument in honour of Carlos Manuel de Céspedes. This lawyer and plantation owner was the initiator of the first Cuban war of independence from 1868 to 1878 *(→History)*. To the rear of the Palacio del Segundo Cabo is the clumsy-looking *Castillo de Real Fuerza* or *La Fuerza* for short. This fortress is one of the oldest Spanish structures in Latin America. After the twenty years it took to build it, the fortress was completed in 1577 and served as the Governor General's residence up to 1762. After the revolution the Nation Library Archives were moved into the building. The roof of the bell tower is crowned by Cuba's trademark: a bronze weather vane called La Giraldilla. This figure is a depiction of Doña Isabell de Bobadilla, the wife of Governor Hernando de Soto. Her main activity was to wait longingly for her husband's return from conquests in new territories. When he died on the far away banks of the Mississippi, she died in Havana of a broken heart.

Plaza de la Catedral. Only a few minutes' walk from Plaza de Armas lies a gem of baroque colonial architecture: the *Cathedral.* A temporary lack of finances resulted in the relatively sombre architecture. Forty years after construction was started, the cathedral with its two bell towers was consecrated in 1789. The façade of limestone is very susceptible to the elements and looks much older than it is. The interior of the cathedral, which is also the final resting place of numerous bishops is only open to the general public weekdays from noon and Sundays 8 to 10 am. The interior is plain, which can be accredited to the fact that it has been remodelled repeatedly over the years. To the left of the church, a plaque marks the former grave site of Cuba's discoverer Christopher Columbus, whose grave was at this site up to 1898.

To the right of the cathedral is the *Palacio del Conde Lombillo;* adjacent to it, the *Palacio de los Marqueses de Arcos.* Both of the buildings date back to the first half of the 18th century. Today, they house offices of the Poder Popular, Cuba's Peoples's Senate *(→ Politics and Government),* and a graphic printing studio. The Palacio de los Condes de Casa Bayona is across from the cathedral. It originates from 1720 and is the oldest building on this square. It is a "Casa señoral" typical of that era with a broad driveway for carriages, a spaciuos patio with a columned entrance in the upper floor and a valuable wooden ceiling. This building has housed the *Museo de Arte Colonial* (Museum of Colonial Art) since 1959. Finally, to the left of the Cathedral is the cozy café and restaurant *La Patio* which has been in operation since 1963. It is in a building which was built in 1760 and was owned by the Marqueses de Aguas Claras for a long time.

La Boguedita del Medio. Only a few yards from the Cathedral on the Calle Emperdrado which branches off is the world famous pub *Bodeguita del Medio* or *B del M* for short. This is simultaneously a restaurant, bar and meeting place. The walls are covered with names and quips. The most famous among this pub's clientele have been immortalised in photos on the walls. Hemingway was a guest here almost every evening; Salvador Allende left behind the witticism "Viva Cuba Libre — Chile espera!" (Long live cuba — Chile wait!). Other famous visitors include Nat King Cole, Francóise Sagan and the Cuban trumpet player Benny Moré. Today, however, it is not the famous artists who fill this pub to overflowing but numerous tourists, black market dealers and ladies of the evening making their rendevous here.

"B del M" is especially famous for Hemingway's favourite drink "Mojito". Bartender Adriano Hernandez is considered the best "Mojito-Mixer" in the country. The food served in "B del M" also has a good reputation and there is no better place than here to make the acquaintance of Cuban cuisine.

Castillo de los Tres Reyes del Morro. The Morro is the oldest Spanish fortification structure in the New World. For 150 years, the fortress was considered impenetrable; however, in 1762, it was conquered by the English after forty four days under siege. Located inside today is a pleasant restaurant; the drawbridge, casemates and moats are worth seeing. One can get to the Morro either through the tunnel leading under the entrance to the harbour or by ferry to the Casablanca district on the opposite shores. From there, it is only a twenty-minute walk to the fortress.

Fortaleza de San Carlos de la Cabaña. Farther inland on the same side, the massive walls of the Cabaña Fortress tower up. Situated atop a knoll, this was already recognised as a strategically important location because whoever could get here with their infantry could easily attack the Morro from here. The English did in fact conquer the Morro and thus the city in 1762. Only a few months after their withdrawal, construction was begun on the Cabaña. However, it would not end up playing a significant role in Havana's defence. During the 19th and 20th centuries, opponents to the regime were executed within these walls. At the end of 1959, rebels under the command of "Che" Guevara conquered the fortress. Since then, the complex has served as a military academy.

Calle Obispo. The residential district surrounding the old "Bishop Street" makes a good example of the layout of newly founded colonial cities dictated by Spain. In order to hold out the heat from the city the streets in southern countries were to be kept narrow – which proves rather troublesome for today's traffic. Maintenance of the old buildings was neglected up until only recently since the government preferred to invest in the rural infrastructure. Meanwhile, the streets of San Ignacio, Obispo, Teriente Rey as well as the two Plaza's have been declared national monuments. The buildings lining them have been restored with the help of UNESCO. Especially beautiful are the "aldabas" which are small door knockers as well as the colourful glass windows in the skylight.

Restaurant El Floridita. *El Floridita* is situated on the corner of Calle Obispo and Avenida Bélgica. The restaurant is famous for its cozy bar. Hemingway immortalised the especially delicious daiquiris here in his work "Islands in the Stream". In memory of the author, these cocktails are served as "Papa Hemingways".

Téatro José Martí, Avenida Bélgica. Built in 1884, the Téatro José Martí was originally conceived as an Opera house. Later the constitutional convention debated here over a new constitution for the independent nation of Cuba. The building has had the name of Téatro José Martí since 1959.

Capitolio Nacional. The capitol in Havana is almost an exact repica of its prototype in Washington. In 1929, it was inaugurated by the dictator Machado after he had employed two thousand workers over twenty years for its construction. As in Washington, the two houses of legislature convene here:

HABANA VIEJA

Legend:
1. Castillo de San Salvador de la Punta ("La Punta")
2. Castillo de los Tres Reyes del Morro
3. El Morro Lighthouse
4. Fortaleza de San Carlos de la Cabana
5. Castillo de la Real Fuerza ("La Fuerza")
6. Plaza de Armas
7. El Templete
8. Palacio del Conde de Santovenia with the "La Flota" Restaurant
9. Palacio de los Capitanes Gencrales
10. Palacio del Segundo Cabo
11. Plaza de la Catedral
12. Palacio de los Marqueses de Aguas Claras with the "El Patio" Restaurant
13. Cathedral
14. Palacio del Conde Lombillo
15. Palacio de los Marqueses de Arcos
16. Palacio de los Condes de Casa Bayon
17. "El Floridita" Restaurant
18. José Martí Theatre
19. Parque de la Fraternidad
20. Capitolio Nacional
21. Felipe Pocy Museum of Natural History
22. Muséo Casa Natal de José Martí
23. Garcia Lorca Theatre
24. Parque 'Central
25. National Museum
26. "Granma" Memorial
27. Revolutionary Museum
28. Corona Cigar Factory

■ Hotels

△
N

0 |—————————————————| 500 m

(map labels)

4

trada del Puerto

e. del Puerto)

5

10   7
9   6   8

Mercaderes

5

Oficios

San Pedro

Plaza
Vieja

Inquisidor

iba

ta

Jesus Maria

namas

Desamparado

the House of Representatives and the Senate. The dome is 94 metres (308) feet) high. In the wing to the left is the *Felipe Poey Museum for Natural History* (→ *Havana/Museums*).

Parque de la Fraternidad. The "Park of Brotherhood" lies across from the capitol and was so named in commeration of the Sixth Panamerican Conference of 1928. The large *Ceiba Tree* at the centre of the park was planted in soil brought from all of the nations.

Paseo de Martí. The Paseo is Havana's showpiece modelled after the Prado in Madrid. It leads from the Capitol straight to the Malecón, the coastal street. The *Téatro Garcia Lorca* lies on the left-hand side after a few minutes' walk from the Capitol. This is home to the National Opera and Ballet. This theatre with box seating can accommodate 2,000 spectators, making it one of the largest of its kind. Directly next to the theatre is Cuba's oldest hotel, the "Inglaterra". Renovated in Moorish style, it is one of the beautiful hotels in Havana. Across from it is the *Parque Central* with a statue of José Martí. Of the other ten monuments of this sort on the island, it differs in that this was the first in Cuba and it was presented to the public by Máximo Gómez, a fellow soldier of Martí in 1908. In the third cross street after the central park is the *Palacio de Bellas Artes,* housing the *National Museum.*

Granma Memorial. The memorial is situated behind the National Museum in a park. The yacht, now within a glass pavillion is a destination for "Granma tourists" from around the world. Eighty-two revolutionaries led by Fidél Castro landed with this yacht on December 2, 1956 in the southern portions of what was then the Oriente province *(→History).*

On display in front of the pavillion are a number of other mementos from this time.

Museum of the Revolution. The Revolution Museum is only a one-minute walk from the Granma Memorial. Appropriately, it is housed in the former Presedential Palace (1920-1960) The exhibitions here offer a thorough overview of the Cuban liberation movement. The photos of the freedom fighters are especially impressive.

The old structure to the left in front of the museum is a remnant of the old city wall which once encircled all of old Havana.

Corona Cigar Factory. This building lies to the right of the Revolution Museum on Calle Zilueta. On several floors, the world famous cigars are rolled by hand, among these are brands like "Romeo y Julieta", "Monte Christo" and "Cohiba". The latter is considered the best brand and even Fidél Castro is said to smoke these. Two additional large cigar factories are also located in Havana. "Partagas" and "H. Upman", both situated directly behind the Capitol on Calle Amistad.

Palacio de Matrimonios. This "Wedding Palace" is located on Paseo Martí only a few steps away from Hotel Inglaterra. It becomes interesting here during the afternoon when the couples to be married pull up in front. And since they all arrive with all of their friends and relatives, it tends to take on the proportions of a small spectacle.

Park of Martyrs. At the end of Avenida de las Missiones, beyond the Revolution Museum it can be seen from the *La Punta Fortress*. The statue of a rider on horseback was erected in honour of Máximo Gómez, one of the most important generals during the war of independence. A few steps farther to the left is a memorial to the medical students. This is a small temple built of marble, the interior of which conceals the remnants of a wall in front of which the eight young medical students were shot to death by Spanish colonial soldiers on November 27, 1871. The charges were the desecration of a Spanish journalists' grave. However their guilt was never proven.

Sights in Habana Moderna

The portion of Modern Havana which is of most interest to tourists includes the district of Vedado and the political centre of Cuba, the *Plaza de la Revolución.*

La Rampa. All of the streets in Vedado are numbered or lettered instead of named. One of the few exceptions to this is the lower segment of the 23rd Street. It is a main traffic artery for the Vedado district, along which most of the hotels, airline offices and shops are located. The Cubans refer to it as simply "La Rampa" and cars do indeed pull down this "ramp" to Malecón, the road along the shores of the bay.

University. The university was founded by the Dominicans in 1728 and it belonged to the Santo Domingo Monastery. It has been in the campus on L Street since 1902. During the colonial period and the pseudo-Republic period *(→History)* the university was a playground for children from wealthy families. The poor and blacks had no access. Since the 1920s an increasing number of patriotically minded students determined the academic scene. During the Batista dictatorship, there were repeated demonstrations and armed campaigns against the regime. Across from the outdoor stairway is the monument to *Antonio Mella* who was spokesman for the patriotically minded students and who also founded the Communist Party of Cuba in 1925. In 1929, he was murdered in Mexican exile.

Museo Antropológico Montané. The museum is located in the building of the "Faculdad de Ciencias, Edificio Felipe Poey" on the university campus. It is one of the museums in Cuba *(→Havana/Museums)*. On display here is an extensive collection of Indian Art.

Museo Napoleónico, Calle Carlitos Aguirre. The Napoleonic Museum is located very near to the university. Of course Napoleon himself was never in

LA HABANA MODERNA
NORTHERN AREA

N
0 ——— 300 m

Legend
1. Julio Antonio Mella Memorial
2. Muséo Antropologico ''Montané''
3. Muséo Napoleónico
4. José Miguel Gómez Memorial

■ Hotels

Bahia de la Habana

Malecón

7

9

11

I

J

K

L

M

N

13

Linea

Ave. Washington

Nacional

Guinol Focsa

O

Capri

N

Victoria

M

15

L

17

K

Humboldt

St. John's

19

J

21

I

23 (Rampa)

Vedado

Habana Libre

H

Colina

1

Calzada de Infanta

Avenida de los Presidentes

25

27 de Noviembre

27

2

Neptuno

27 de Noviembre

Universität

3

La Habana

Ronda

Mazón

Basarrate

F

Hospital Gen.

E

23

Calixto García

Aguire

Valle

H. Upmant

D

Stadion

C

Juan Abrantes

4

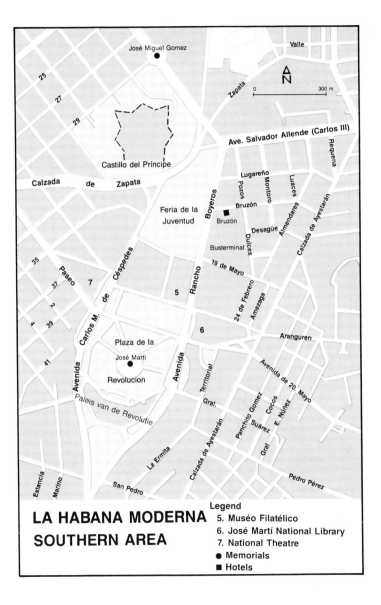

José Miguel Gomez

Valle

25

27

29

Zapata

N

0   300 m

Castillo del Príncipe

Ave. Salvador Allende (Carlos III)

Requena

Calzada   de   Zapata

Lugareño

Boyeros

Pozos

Montoro

Luaces

Feria de la
Juventud

■ Bruzón

Almendares

Calzada de Ayestarán

Bruzón

Desagüe

Dulces

Busterminal

35

Paseo

7

Céspedes

19 de Mayo

37

5

Rancho

2

Carlos M. de

24 de Febrero

Amezaga

4

39

6

Aranguren

41

Plaza de la

Avenida

José Marti

Territorial

Avenida de 20. Mayo

Avenida

Revolucion

Gral.

Panchito Gomez

Cocos

E. Núñez

Paleis van de Revolutie

La Ermita

Calzada de Ayestarán

Gral.

Estancia

Marino

San Pedro

Pedro Pérez

LA HABANA MODERNA
SOUTHERN AREA

Legend
5. Muséo Filatélico
6. José Martí National Library
7. National Theatre
● Memorials
■ Hotels

Cuba, however the sugar baron Julio Lobo was a fan of Napoleon and collected everything that had anything that had to do with the short emperor: paintings, Gobelins, porcelain pieces, weapons and tapestries. The villa erected in Florentine style was specially built to house this collection.

Plaza de la Revolución, Avenida de la Independencia. This square is the focal point of Modern Havana and the political hub of Cuba. Its western side is bordered by the Governmental Palace, the seat of the Central Committee of the Cuban Communist Party. Directly opposite is the Ministry of Domestic Affairs, easily recognised by the massive portrait of "Che" Guevara on the front façade. To the left of this building are the *National Library* and the *Ministry of Defence*. Be careful when taking pictures here!

The *José Martí Monument* towers up at the centre of this square. This obelisk is 152 metres (497 feet) in height. Located at its base is a memorial hall where Martí's words can be read immortalised in green marble. "Human rights are not obtained through tears, but blood." The Plaza de la Revolución is the Cuban pendant to the Tiananmen Square in Peking or Moscow's Red Square: Fidél Castro held his May 1st speech here. The National Library has over one million books and is visited by over 500,000 Cubans annually.

Cementrio de Cristóbol Colón, (Christopher Columbus Cemetery), Calzada de Zapata. The cemetery is located near *Plaza de la Revolución*. It counts among the world's most beautiful cemeteries due to its wealth of gravestones. This cemetery was laid out in 1871. The tree-lined boulevard leading to the chapel is lined with the majority of the most significant graves in terms of cultural history. With a total of 800,000 graves and almost 100,000 crypts, this is the largest cemetery in Latin America.

Havana / **Practical Information**

Accommodation

(For general information →*Accommodation*)

Upper Price Category

Habana Libre, Vedado, Calle L y 23, Tel: 30-5011. Double rooms are priced from $72 (£42). The former Havana Hilton, once the provisional headquarters of the rebel army is the largest hotel in the city and is a city unto itself, equipped with everything the heart could desire.

Habana Riviera, Avenida Malecón y Avenida Paseo, Vedado, Tel: 30-5051. Double rooms are priced from $80 (£47). Financed by the mafia at the time it was built this luxury hotel has an American style and standards. It includes a swimming pool and the "Copa Room" night club with live music.

Capri, Calle 21 y N, Vedado, Tel: 52-0511, with double rooms from $60 (£35); furnished as above, swimming pool, "Cabaret Capri".

Nacional, Calle O y 21, Vedado, Tel: 7-8981, double rooms from $152 (£89). An impressive luxury hotel built in the colonial architectural style with a turbulent past. In 1933, the entire government and the military barricaded themselves in the *Nacional* from the revolting masses. In 1946, a birthday party for Frank Sinatra took place, organised by the mafia bosses Meyer-Lanski and "Lucky" Luciano. Today, the bar area was once one of the most exclusive gambling casinos in Havana. The hotel has a swimming pool and also "Cabaret Parisien". Hotel Nacional was completely renovated in 1992.

Inglaterra, Paseo Martí, entre Boulevard San Rafael y Neptuno, Centro Habana (at the central park), Tel: 6-6181, double rooms from $60 (£35). A beautiful old building in colonial style and ideal as a base for exploring Habana Vieja. Restaurant and a bar with a rooftop terrace, recommended.

Sevilla, Trocadero No. 55, entre Paseo de Martí y Zulueta, Centro Habana, Tel: 6-9961, double rooms from $84 (£49). A well maintained old building near the Prado.

Plaza, Avenida Agramonte (or Zulueta) No. 267, Tel: 61-8306, double rooms from $72 (£42). A renovated Spanish building at Parque Central.

Middle Price Category

Colina, Calle L y 27, Vedado, Tel: 32-3535, double rooms from $33 (£20). Friendly staff and clean, restaurant and bar.

Deauville, Avenida de Italia No. 1, entre Malecón y San Lazaro, Centro Habana near the old city district, Tel: 61-6901; double rooms from $38 (£23). Restaurant, bar, cafeteria and swimming pool.

St. John's, Calle O, entre 23 y Humboldt, Vedado, Tel: 32-9531; double rooms from $36 (£21). Clean, centrally located hotel. Swimming pool on the roof. Nightclubs: "El Pico Blanco" and "Rincon del Feeling".

Vedado, Calle O, entre Humboldt y 25, Vedado, Tel: 32-6501; double rooms from $44 (£26). Centrally located with a swimming pool and bar/restaurant.

Inexpensive Hotels

New York, Calle Dragones No. 156, Centro Habana, Tel: 61-7938, around $25 (£15). An acceptable hotel within sight of the capitol.

Caribbean, Paseo de Martí No. 164, near Habana Vieja, Tel: 80-4975, double rooms from $21 (£13). Not very pretty from the outside but acceptable inside.

Bruzón, Calle Bruzón No. 217, Tel: 70-9388, directly at the Terminal de Omnibus Interprovinciales. Only recommended for this reason.

Packard, near Habana Vieja, Paseo de Martí No. 51, Tel: 61-5901. Not the best looking from the outside and not inside either, but clean.

Activities

There is always something to do or something going on in Havana. The theatre and opera, art galleries, cinemas, bars and revue cabarets, outdoor dance performances and countless discotheques (called "cabarets" in Havana) provide diversion and ensure that one will never succumb to boredom. One can find out exactly what is happening where in the hotels or in the *Office for Individual Tourism* in the *Havana Libre* Hotel.

Popular places for special events are the Plaza de Armas in Habana Vieja, the Parque Central and the stage in the inner courtyard of the Casa de Cultura on Calle N between Calle 21 and 23 in Varadero.

In the cabaret *Beach Club* in the *Habana Riviera* Hotel, live performances take place every evening with a dance group and an orchestra. The *Casa de las Américas* on Avenida de los Presidentes offers poetry readings, concerts and theatre performances on a regular basis. *Café Cantante* in the *Teátro Nacional* is a meeting place for the younger crowd.

Every Saturday: Sábado de Rumba, the "Rumba Saturday", begins around 2 pm in the inner courtyard of the *Conjunto Folclórico Nacional* which is known throughout Cuba. Members of the ensemble and students dance the original form of the Rumba for a predominantly black audience. The director explains each dance and the figures beforehand so that one can learn about African mythology. Those who would like to are welcome to join in the dance. Vedado, Calle 4, entre Calzada y Linea.

Traditional folk music is performed during the weekend in the "Casa de Trova", San Lazaro, No. 661. Both young and old musicians meet here for turbulent jam sessions.

Sábado de los Libros, the "Book Sunday" is held by the *La Moderna Poesia* bookshop. Famous Cuban authors often read their newest works during the afternoon. *Sábado de la Plaza:* on Plaza de Armas as well as on Plaza de la Catedral there are large handicrafts markets held every Saturday. In addition to painters and sculptors, there are also a number of musicians and dancers who meet here. The result is often spontaneous performances.

Mondays: A reminder of the proportion of African descendants in the population are the Afro-Cuban evenings. The *noche afrocubaná* in the greater Havana region only on Mondays around 9 pm in the Finca Justiz near Santa María. The trip there and back is provided by Cubatur *(→Travel in Cuba / Cubatur).* Spectators will experience a living piece of African culture, learning dances and rituals as well as getting to know the various cults as they were practised by the black slaves on the sugar plantations.

Arriving at the Airport

There are two shuttle services from the José Martí Airport into the city. Tour groups are brought to their hotels in buses chartered by Cubatur *(→Travel in Cuba / Cubatur).* Those travelling individually must take a taxi or the bus. Payment is made in pesos. The bus stop is located on the opposite side of the street in front of the airport. Bus line 31 takes passengers into the city; however, one must change buses in Vibora and take the 68. This will take passengers directly to Vedado. The bus trip takes around an hour and is quite often rather strenuous. The taxis only require a half an hour for the same route. When going back to the airport for the return flight, one should not opt for the bus because these can be rather unreliable at times. Definitely take a taxi. One should arrive at the airport two hours before the scheduled departure for all international flights.

Art Galleries

The new government saw one of the most important endeavours of the takeover in 1959 as bringing art to the people. This policy was apparently successful: the galleries are always well frequented in Cuba, in contrast to other countries since they appeal to the normal consumer and encourage people to be artistically active themselves.

The exhibitions are mainly concentrated on contemporary art (sculptures, paintings, graphics and folk art). *Galería de la Plaza* and *Galería Grabado,* Plaza de la Catedral, Habana Vieja. *Galería Centro del Arte Internacional,* Calle San Rafael No. 105, Centro Habana. *Galería de la Casa de Cultura,* Calzada y 8, Vedado. *Galería de La Habana,* Linea No. 462, corner of F, Vedado. *Galería Latinoamericana,* Casa de las Américas, Calle G y 3, second floor, Vedado. These galleries are open Tuesday to Saturday from 2 to 3 and 6 to 10 pm; closed Mondays.

Beaches

The fabulous beaches to the east of Havana are grouped under the name *Playas del Este.* Individually, these include:

Playa Bacuranao, Celimar. 15 kilometres (9 miles) from Havana and situated on a small bay with the ruins of a Spanish watchtower within view.

Accommodation: *Villa Bacuranao* (directly on the beach), Tel: 087-4431. The "cabañas" are somewhat older but are equipped with a bathroom, toilet, a telephone and air conditioning. Double rooms are available starting at $29 (£17). There is also a good restaurant and the complex also has a car and bicycle rental agency.

Playa Mégano, 22 kilometres (14 miles) from Havana.

Accommodation: *Villa Mégano,* near the beach, Tel: 077-4441. All of the "cabañas" have a bathroom and toilet, a telephone and air conditioning. Double rooms start at $29 (£17). The complex includes a restaurant, a café, a swimming pool, tennis courts and a shop.

Playa Santa María del Mar, This is the most beautiful and heavily frequented beach.

Accommodation: Hotel *Marazul,* Avenida Terrazas y Calle 7, Tel: 087-2531. This is the largest and most expensive hotel in the area. Double rooms from $38 (£23). Hotel *Atlántico,* Avenida Terrazas y Calle 11, Tel: 087-2551. A quaint and cozy little hotel with twenty comfortable rooms from $32 (£19). It is usually completely booked well in advance so make reservations early. *Villa Los Pinos,* Avenida Terrazas y Calle 21, Tel: 087-2571. This holiday settlement is situated in a very idyllic location in a pine forest and has bungalows with up to six bedrooms. The standard appointments include: bathroom, toilet, air conditioning, telephone, radio, television and a refrigerator. Rooms are available from $40 (£24).

Restaurants in Santa María: *Restaurante-Bar Caribe,* Avenida Terrazas y Calle 13, open from noon to midnight, serving Cuban and international cuisine. *El Trópico,* Calle 9, entre Avenida Terrazas y Avenida del Sur. Good value!

Entertainment: *Centro Nocturno Habana Club,* Calle 10, entre 1 y 3, Tel: 3384, open daily from 7 pm to 3 am. *Cabaret Pino del Mar,* Avenida del Sur, entre 5 y 7, Tel: 2729, open Tuesday to Sunday from 8 until midnight.

Playa Guanabo, a very nice beach and quite popular especially during the main Cuban holiday season. Most of the inexpensive hotels are completely booked long in advance during this time of year.

Accommodation: Hotel *Las Avenidas,* Calle 478, entre 3 y 5. Hotel *Miramar,* Calle 478, entre 78 y 9. Hotel *Gran Via,* Avenida 5 y 462. Hotel *María,* Avenida 5 entre 472 y 474, Tel: 087-2774. An extensive complex with 102 simple "cabañas", swimming pool, a restaurant and sports facilities; priced from $25 (£15).

Restaurants in Guanabo: there are numerous cafeterias and snack bars directly on the beach and along Avenida 5. More elegant restaurants include the *Belic,* Avenida 5 y Calle 478 and the *Guanabo Club,* Calle 468, entre 13 y 15.

Playa Jibacoa, the westernmost beach the farthest away from Havana (60 kilometres/38 miles), framed in rugged cliffs.

Accommodation: *Camping Jibacoa,* tents are rented out or one can choose a simple cottage. $10 (£6) per person. Meals are available in the camping area. The camp's offices are open daily from 9 am to 4:45 pm. Diving masks and boats are available as are horses for a ride along the beach.

Villa Loma, Santa Cruz del Norte (Playa Jibacoa). Opened in 1978 and comprising 23 small and several large "cabañas", this holiday complex has a restaurant, a bar and a cafeteria. Prices start at $35 (£21). There are also numerous sports facilities.

Important Tip: Running parallel to the road to Mantanzas there is a coastal road to Playa Arroyo Bermejo.

Accommodation: *Villa El Trópico,* priced from $35 (£21). There is a supplies centre as well as sport facilities.

Around 2 kilometres (1 mile) before reaching the *Villa El Trópico,* the holiday settlement *El Abra* was opened only a few years ago. Its 250 simple "cabañas" are all equipped with a bathroom and toilet. A cottage for three people costs around $20 (£12).

Cubatur offers day-long excursions to all of these beaches. The municipal buses to _Bacuranao_ as well as _Santa María del Mar_ and _Guanabo_ depart from Parque Central: bus lines 62, 162 and 262.

There is one rule of thumb valid for all the _Playas del Este:_ The farther from the capital city the less crowded and hectic the beaches are. The most bustling beaches are Santa María and Guanabo. During the weekends, it is only possible to find some peace and quiet beyond Santa Cruz del Norte.

Bookstores

Those interested in Latin American literature should pay a visit to the _La Moderna Poesia_ book store. In addition to classics from the continent, one will also find works by less widely known authors. All of the books are relatively inexpensive. On Saturdays, readings take place here regularly _(→Practical Information/Activities)_. Next door is the _Máximo Gorki_ bookstore offering Russian literature. The Intur shops in all of the larger hotels also have a selection of books, usually novels and childrens books _(→Shopping)_.

Car Rental

Branch offices of havanautos can be found at the airport (Agencia Aeropuerto "José Martí", Tel: 5-683-3007 or -3052), in Hotel _Capri_ (Tel: 32-6484 or 32-0511), in Hotel _Triton_ (Tel: 2-6921) and Hotel _Riviera_ (Tel: 30-5051).

Cinemas

The most important of the 170 cinemas in Havana include: _Acapulco,_ Calle 26, entre 36 y 37, Nuevo Vedado. _Cine 12 y 23,_ Calle 12 y 23, Vedado. _Cinemateca,_ Calle 23 entre 10 y 12, Vedado. _La Rampa,_ Calle 23, entre O y P, Vedado. _Olympic,_ Calle Linéa, entre B y C, Vedado. _Riviera,_ Calle 23, entre H y G, Vedado. _Trianón,_ Calle 23, entre Paseo y A, Vedado. _Yara,_ Calle 23 y L, Vedado. _Payset,_ Paseo de Martí y San José, Habana Vieja. _América,_ Calle Galiano, entre Concordia y Neptuno, Centro Habana. _Rialto,_ Calle Neptuno, corner of Paseo de Martí.

Excursions

Lenin Park, Calle 100 y Cortina de la Presa, Arroyo Naranjo, Tel: 44-3027, 44-4344, 44-3060. A recreation area southwest of the city. It is best to take a taxi.

Cojimar (→Cojimar). One can get to this fishing village by taxi or bus number 58 from Calle Monte near the Capitol.

Playas del Este (→Practical Information/Beaches)

Museums

Cuba's government view the history not as a collection of facts and dates but as a key to understanding the present. The presentation of the Cuban battle for independence _(→History)_ is given a broad scope. The museums are lovingly set up with attention to detail and the staff is extremely happy to provide information. Photography is not allowed; admission is free of charge. All of the museums are closed Mondays.

Museo de la Revolución (Museum of the Revolution) Calle Refugio entre Zulueta y Avenida de las Missiones, Centro Habana, Tel: 68849. The museum in the former Presidential Palace provides an informative overview of the Cuban people's battle for independence up to 1959 through photos, documents, weapons and personal articles. Open Tuesday to Friday from 12:30 to 8 pm; Saturdays and Sundays from 11:30 am to 5 pm.

Memorial "Granma", on the square between the Museo de la Revolución and the Palacio de Artes in Centro Habana. In the centre of this green rondelle is the legendary "Granma" yacht in a glass pavillion and guarded day and night by an honourary guard. It is open during the same times as the Museo de la Revolución.

Museo Casa Natal de José Martí (House where José Martí was born), Calle Leonor Pérez No. 14 near the train station, Habana Vieja, Tel: 68852. José Martí (1853-1895), the proponent of Cuba's independence, was born in this house and he also spent his childhood here. On display here are documents,

"Sabado de Rumba" at Havana's "Vedado" Hotel: music and dance are an integral part of the Cuban culture

photographs and excerpts from his philosophical, pedagogical and revolution-ary writings. Open Tuesday to Sunday from 1:30 to 8:30 pm.

Museo Casa de Abel Santamaria, Calle 25 No. 164, Apto. 601, entre Infanta y O, Vedado, Tel: 71179. Fidél Castro met with the revolutionaries of the 1950s in Abel Santamaria's small apartment. Open Tuesday to Saturday from 9 am to 5 pm; Sunday from 9 am to 1 pm.

Museo de la Ciudad de la Habana (Municipal Museum of Habana), Calle Tacón No. 1, entre Obispo y O'Reilly in the Palacio de los Capitanes Gener-ales, Habana Vieja, Tel: 610722. Since there are a number of items originating from Spain in this museum it becomes very apparent that Havana's history was most strongly influenced by the Spanish colonial history. The museum is sometimes used for cultural events. Open Tuesday to Saturday from 3 to 6 and 7 to 9 pm; Sundays from 9 am to 1 pm.

Museo de Armas (Weapons Museum), Calle O'Reilly y Avenida del Puerto (in the Castillo de la Fuerza), Habana Vieha, Tel: 800216. With just which weapons the people used from the beginning of history to the 19th century to kill each other can be seen in this museum. Open Tuesday to Saturday from 11 am to 7 pm; Sundays from 8 am to noon.

Museo Napoleónico (Napoleonic Museum), Calle San Miguel, No. 1159, entre Mázon y Ronda (near the university), Vedado, Tel: 791412. The sugar baron Julio Lobo was an enthusiastic collector of objects having to do with Napoleon and the era in which he lived. The beautiful villa was built in 1928 especially for the exhibition of these articles. Open Tuesday to Saturday from 1:30 to 8:30 pm; Sundays from 9 am to noon.

Museo del Pueblo Combatiente (Museum of the combating people), Avenida 5 and Calle 72, Miramar. Set up in the former Peruvian embassy, the permanent exhibition here documents the counterrevolutionary attacks on the Cuban facilities and focuses on the problem of emigrating Cubans during the 1960s. Open Tuesday to Saturday from 3 to 10 pm; Sundays from 10 am to 6 pm.

Museo Antropológico "Montané" (Anthropological Museum), Calle 27, Univer-sity de La Habana, Facultad de Ciencias, Edificio "Felipe Poey", second floor, Vedado, Tel: 329000. Exhbitions on pre-Columbian culture in Cuba. Open Monday to Friday from 9 am to noon and 2 to 5 pm; closed Saturdays and Sundays.

Museo Histórico de Guanabacoa (Historical Museum of Guanabacoa), Calle Martí, No. 108, entre San Antonio y Versalles, Municipio Guanagacoa, Tel: 909117. In 33 exhibition rooms, this beautiful museum documents predomi-nantly those elements of Cuban Culture which were brought into the country by the African slaves as well as important events which took place in this region like the British invasion and the tedious struggle of the Cuban people for independence. Open Tuesday to Saturday from 4 to 10 pm; Sundays from 2 to 6 pm.

Museo Hemingway, Finca Vigía/Steinbarts, San Francisco de Paula. The famous author Ernest Hemingway welcomed the takeover of Fidél Castro and for this reason is very popular in Cuba even today. He bought the villa "Finca La Vigía" in 1940 and lived there until 1960, when he transferred its ownership to the Cuban government. The government has changed nothing inside with the exception of the necessary renovations. Even the unopened letters are still in the entryway as well as Hemingway's books still being in the living room – as if he just stepped out to the "Bodeguita del Medio"... Open Tuesday to Saturday from 9 am to noon and 1 to 5 pm; Sundays from 9 am to 1 pm.

Museo Numismatico (Numismatic Museum), Calle Aguiar, No. 456, entre Amargura y Lamparilla, Habana Vieja, Tel: 66578. Open Tuesday to Saturday from 3 to 9 pm; Sundays from 9 am to noon.

Museo Postal Filatélico (Philatelic Museum), Ministeria de Communicaciones, Plaza de la Revolución y Avenida de la Independencia, Vedado, Tel: 705193. Stamp collectors will enjoy a visit here: the collection on display documents the history of the Cuban postal system and visitors can even buy a few souvenirs here. Open Wednesday to Friday from 10 am to 6 pm; Saturdays from 10 am to 2 pm.

Museo Nacional (National Museum), Calle Trocadero y Zulueta, Palacio de Bellas Artes, Centro Habana, Tel: 613915 or 68198. In the National Museum, visitors will gain insight into Cuban contemporary painting but also into the art of times gone by. Open Tuesday to Saturday from 1:30 to 8:30 pm; Sundays from 9 am to noon.

Museo de Arte Colonial (Museum of Colonial Art), Calle San Ignacio, No. 61 (Plaza de la Catedral), Habana Vieja, Tel: 611367. Open Tuesday to Saturday from 1:30 to 8:30 pm; Sundays from 9 am to noon.

Museo de Artes Decorativas (Museum of the Decorative Arts), Calle 17, No. 502, entre Calle D y E, Vedado, Tel: 321300. Chinese, Japanese and French decorative and applied arts from the 18th and 19th centuries collected by Cuban millionaires who fled Cuba to Miami in 1959. Open Tuesday to Saturday from 1:30 to 8:30 pm; Sundays from 9 am to noon.

Museo de la Alfabetización (Museum of Literacy), Ciudad Libertad, Marianao, Tel: 208054. At the beginning of the 1960s, the illiteracy rate in Cuba was still very high. The new government under Fidél Castro took steps to combat this problem. Open Tuesday to Saturday from 9:30 to 11:30 am and 2 to 6 pm; closed Saturdays and Sundays. The museum can only be visited if taking an organised tour through Cubatur.

Museo y Archivo de la Musica (Museum and Archives for the History of Music), Calle Capdevila No. 1, entre Aguiar y Habana, Centro Habana, Tel: 806810.

Exhibitions covering the development of various Cuban musical styles. Open Tuesday to Saturday from 10 am to 6 pm; Sundays from 8 am to noon.

Museo de Ciencias Naturales "Felipe Poey" ("Felipe Poey" Museum of Natural Sciences), Paseo Martí y San José, Capitolio Nacional (entrance left of the stairway), Centro Habana, Tel: 800707. Here, one can see the earliest Columbian cliff paintings from the Punta del Este Cave. Open Tuesday to Saturday from 2 to 9 pm; Sundays from 9:30 am to 12:30 pm.

Museo de Ciencias "Carlos Finlay" ("Carlos Finlay" Museum of Sciences), Calle Cuba No. 460, entre Amargura y Teniente Rey, Habana Vieja, Tel: 68006. One can see what the most brilliant Cuban minds brought to paper here – only the fewest of the visitors will understand it though. Open Monday to Friday from 8 am to noon and 1 to 5 pm; closed Saturdays and Sundays.

Detailed information on modern-day Cuba is available at the *Pabellón Cuba* on La Rampa between N and M. A photographic documentation of achievements and advances since 1959 is also on display here.

Night Life

The warm nights of Havana are just ideal for a long tour of the pubs – if one does not stick to the hotel bars. The casinos, striptease bars and bordellos disappeared with the US dominance in Cuba and with them all of the glittering night life. The bars and the large revue shows did remain since music, dancing and rum are simply inseparable from Cuba. And: every establishment is open to all Cubans and the prices are affordable.

One word on *terminology:* "Cabarets" are nightclubs and not cabarets in the classic sense. Almost every tourist hotels will have one. Professional show bands and pretty dancers in risqué costumes provide for an electric atmosphere. There are usually two shows per evening. During weekends, one must reserve seats in the better cabarets.

"Clubs" are intimate bars with subdued red lighting, predominantly frequented by couples. The music is both live and from recordings.

"Centros nocturnos" are discotheques with light shows.

The most famous cabaret in Havana and a definite must for every visitor is the *Tropicana,* Calle 72, entre 43 y Linea, Marianao, Tel: 24544 or 66224, open Tuesday to Sunday from 8 pm to 3 am with the show beginning around 11 pm. Closed Monday. An evening out at the *Tropicana* costs around $40 (£24) including transportation there, admission and two drinks. This price also includes an excellent show well into the wee hours of the morning – both colourful and lively. The excursion to the *Tropicana* around 25 minutes from the *Habana Libre* is organised by Cubatur. One can also take the bus no. 22 almost to the front door; Admission is then around $25 (£15) including one drink.

A small selection of a total of 33 cabarets and nightclubs: *Cabaret Copa, Hotel Habana Riviera,* Paseo y Malecón, Vedado, Tel: 305051, open 9 pm to 2 am; closed Wednesdays. *Cabaret Parisien,* Hotel *Nacional,* Calle 21 y O, Vedado, Tel: 78981, closed Tuesdays. Cabaret *Capri,* Hotel *Capri,* Calle 21 y L, Vedado, Tel: 320511, closed Mondays. *Atelier,* Calle 17 y 6 Vedado, Tel: 37144. *Barbaram,* Calle 26 y 27, Vedado, Tel: 317411. *Johnny's 88,* Calle 15, entre N y O, Vedado, Tel: 323143. *Karachi,* Calle 17 y K, Vedado, Tel: 322037. *La Gruta,* Calle 23, entre O y P, Vedado, Tel: 78410. *Pico Blanco,* Calle O, entre 23 y 25, Vedado, Tel: 329531. *Rincon Bohemió,* Calle M, entre 17 y 19, Vedado, Tel: 324471. *Scheherezade,* Calle 19 y M, Vedado, Tel: 325736. *Tikoa,* Calle 23, entre N y O, Vedado, Tel: 323151.

Post and Telephone

There is a post office in the Hotel *Habana Libre.* One can place international calls to Europe either here or at one of the other larger hotels. Three minutes to Europe costs around $6 (£4). For sending letters to Cuba, one should note the following address for general delivery:

Name
Avenida Rancho Boyeros y 19 de Mayo
Ministerio Communicaciones
Habana 6
Cuba/Correo aereo (air mail)

The names of the people who have received mail are posted.

Local calls can be made from the telephones here, costing 5 centavos.

Restaurants

Havana has a large number of restaurants worth visiting. Reservations are necessary during the weekend. Reservations can be made at the hotel reception or in the *Office for Individual Tourism* in Havana Libre *(→Cuisine).*
In the restaurants frequented by tourists, payment is expected in US dollars. The prices for first-class restaurants range from $25 to $30 (£15 to £18) per person and from $10 to $15 (£6 to £9) for restaurants in the middle category. In addition, there are usually buffets in the larger hotels both during lunchtime and in the evening. One can eat well here without having to make advance reservations. Rationing is slightly noticeable at some times but this does not impede an enjoyable evening.

Those who would like to spend less on meals should visit the cafeterias and pizzerias. One should count on waiting quite a while for a seat.

Vedado

Los Andes, Calle 21, No. 52, corner of M, Tel: 320383. Cuban Cuisine.

La Arboleda in Hotel Nacional, Tel: 78981; a restaurant serving buffets, overlooking the sea.

El Cochinito, Calle 23 No. 457, entre I y H, Tel: 404501. Speciality: pork.

El Conejito, Calle M No. 206, corner of 17, Tel: 705001. A restaurant in British Tudor style. Speciality: chicken.

El Mandarin, Calle O No. 34, entre N y M, Tel: 320677. Chinese.

Monseñor, Calle O No. 120, entre 21 y O, Tel: 329884. International Cuisine.

Moscú, Calle P, entre Humboldt y 23, Tel: 796571. Russian Cuisine.

Polinesio, Calle L y 23, in the Hotel Habana Libre, Tel: 323753. Asian and South Pacific specialities.

Restaurante 1830, Calzada 1252 near the Almendares Tunnel, Tel: 36954. There are three salons in this building: the Restaurant *Tropicana* as well as lively bars with a view of the Atlantic. International and Cuban cuisine.

La Roca, Calle 21 No. 102, corner of M, Tel: 328698. Cozy, serving international and Cuban cuisine.

Sierra Maestra, in the hotel *Habana Libre,* Tel: 30511. Upper floor.

Sofía, Calle O corner of 23. Good Bulgarian food.

La Torre, Calle 17 No. 55 corner of M, Tel: 324630. A pleasant restaurant at the top of the "Focsa" building, serving international cuisine with a view over the city.

Tropicana dancers in today's Cuba - the popular dance rythms have their roots in African music

Yang Tse, Calle 23 corner of 26, serving Asian cuisine of inconsistent quality.
Habana Vieja
La Bodeguita del Medio, Calle Empedrado No. 207, Tel: 66121. Cuban
Cuisine.
La Casa de los Vinos, Calle Esperanza 1, corner of Factoría, Tel: 610073.
Spanish cuisine and everyday dishes away from the bustle of the tourist
centres.
Méson de la Flota, Baratillo No. 9, Plaza de Armas. Cuban cuisine inside a
building from the Spanish colonial period. Open from 11 am to 2 pm.
El Patio, Calle San Ignacio No. 54, Plaza de la Catedral, Tel: 614550. Cuban
cuisine in a pleasant atmosphere.
El Restaurante Floridita, Avenida Bélgica No. 353 corner of Obispo, Tel:
612932. An evening restaurant with musical entertainment. Specialities: fish
and seafood.
El Colmao, Calle Aramburu No. 366, entre San Rafael y San José, Centro
Habana, Tel: 701113.
Meson La Chorrero, Malecón No 20 near the Almendares Tunnel, Vedado,
Tel: 34504; open 6 pm to 1 am, closed Mondays.
Taberna Castillo San Salvador de la Punta, Malecón y Paseo de Martí, Centro
Habana, Tel: 66001, open from 6 pm to 1 am; closed Mondays.
Taberna Castillo Los Tres Reyes del Morro, Carretera de la Cabana, Habana
del Este, Tel: 65129, open from 5 pm to 1 am; closed Mondays.
Inexpensive Restaurants, Cafeterias and Pizzerias
Cafeteria Hotel Sevilla, Centro Habana.
Wakamba, Vedado, Calle O across from Hotel St. John's.
Lafayette, Calle Aguiar, entre Calle Progreso y Calle O'Reilly near Plaza de
la Catedral.
Marakas, Calle O, entre 23 y 25, Vedado.
Pio-Pio Restaurant, Calle L, entre 15 y 17 near Calle O'Reilly.
Pizzeria Milán, Calle 23 y P, Vedado.
Prado 264, Prado No. 264.

Shopping
There are various alternatives for shopping in Havana. In the Intur shops one
can not only buy everything one needs for US dollars, but typically Cuban
products and souvenirs as well. The largest hotels are the Intur shops with
the best selection. The shop in Hotel *Vedado* has the best selection of records
and cassette tapes. Cuban handicrafts are best purchased in the *Galería
Grábado* on Plaza de Armas and in the *Palacio de Artesánia,* Calle Cuba No.
1664.
Cubans buy their records on Calle Monserrate for example, the shopping area
of Manzana de Gómez or at Calle San Miguel No. 410 at EGREM. The largest

proportion of tourists buy the typically Cuban folk music called "musica tradicional". The most widely known artists for this type of music are: Conjunto Folclórico Nacional (Afro-Cuban music), Conjunto Palmas y Cañas, Los Montunos, Duo Los Compadres, Joseito Fernandez, Carlos Puebla. Modern Cuban dance music: Irakere, Los Van-Van, Son 14, Rumbavana, Grupo Moncada.

In the *Centro* store on Plaza de la Fraternidad, one can obtain information on what goods are available. Smaller shops can still be found on Calle Oficios in the Convento de San Francisco de Asisi in Habana Vieja.

Tours of the City

Cubatur offers a number of interesting tours of the city with thematic focus. They begin and end at Hotels *Habana Libre, Habana Riviera, Nacional, Capri, Deauville, Vedado* and *St. John's*. They are conducted by a multi-lingual tour guide and can be booked in the hotels mentioned above. The tours last around 2 hours.

Theatres and Concert Halls

Information on the current calendar of events can be found in the weekly edition of newspapers under the heading "Cartelera Cultural" (available in the tourist offices at the hotels) as well as through Cubatur. There are eight state run stages in Havana as well as a puppet theatre.

Teátro García Lorca, Paseo de Martí y San Rafael, Centro Habana, Tel: 622700.

Alicia Alonso, who is the director of the National Ballet is among the most respected personalities in Cuba. *Teatro Nacional,* Paseo y 37, Vedado, Tel: 74655. One can enjoy very good performances by visiting foreign theatre ensembles here.

Teatro José Martí, Calle Dragones, entre Paseo y Agramonte, Habana Vieja, Tel: 806037.

Teatro Carlos Marx, Calle 1 y 10, Vedado, Tel: 38282. The programme in this theatre includes performances from all performing genres.

Teatro Hubert de Blanck, Calzada, entre A y B, Vedado, Tel: 320660. Modern pieces by dramatists of various nationalities are premiered here.

Teatro Julio Mella, Línea, entre A y B, Vedado, Tel: 38696.

Teatro El Sótano, Calle K, entre 25 y 27, Vedado, Tel: 320630.

Teatro Musical, Calle Consulado y Virtudes, Centro Habana, Tel: 614986.

Teatro Nacional de Guinol, Calle M, entre 17 y 19, Vedado, Tel: 326262. This is a puppet theatre for the smaller theatre-goers.

Tourist Information

Cubatur, on the "Rampa", Calle 23, No. 156, Ciudad de Habana 4, Tel: 32-4521, Telex TURCU 511 243. Those travelling on their own can find the *Office for Individual Tourism* in *Hotel Habana Libre.*

Transportation

Municipal Buses

As every visitor to Havana will quickly notice, the city has a dense network of public transportation. The buses, called "guagua" (say: wah-wah) are usually filled to overflowing and zip back and forth. The only thing is that there seems to be no way of knowing which bus goes where and no Habanero can say either for certain. Thus, most of the local residents only know which direction "their bus" takes until it reaches "their" stop. The stressful rush-hours are between 7 and 10 am as well as from 3 to 6 pm. The following are some of the bus lines. These all depart from Vedado. Beginning at 11 pm, the buses only operate every half hour. It is difficult to get a taxi during the evening hours. If one is in the old city centre during the evening then it best to go out to Malecón where there are usually a number of taxis.

Vedado →Habana Vieja: from Calle M between 25 y 27: 27, 227; also from Coppelia, Calle 23 y L, down to Malecón: 64, 98, 195 (the 64 continues to "Estación Central").

Vedado →Miramar: from Coppelia, inland: 32, 132.

Vedado →Marianao: from Coppelia, inland: 22.

Vedado →Nuevo Vedado: from Calle Jovellar near the University: 84 (stops at the Terminal de Omnibus Interprovinciales).

Vedado →Airport: from Calle O y 21 across from Hotel Nacional: 68 to Vibora, then transfer to the 31.

From Habana Vieja back to Vedado, from:

Calle Cuba y Espada, near La Punta: 98, 227.

Avenido del Puerto near La Fuerza: 82, 98.

Calle Animas between Paseo de Martí and Calle Zulueta: 22, 64, 132.

Cross-Country Buses

All of the buses to other provinces depart from the "Terminal de Omnibus Interprovinciales", Avenida de la Indepencia, Vedado. One must make reservations several days in advance since the buses are so inexpensive and a very popular means of travel in Cuba *(→Travel in Cuba)*. Reservations must be made at the bus terminal or in the Buró de Reservaciones, Calle 21 y 4, Vedado. An hour befor departure is the latest that one should arrive at the bus terminal since the tickets are otherwise sold to people on the waiting list.

Train Travel

From Havana's three train stations, trains depart to just about every direction. It does become difficult during the summer months because half of Cuba seems to be on holiday. Make reservations well in advance. Tickets can be purchased directly at the train stations and be sure to check-in early because the waiting list system is in effect here as well.

Trains to the eastern portions of Cuba depart from the "Estación Central", Calle Egido, Habana Vieja. The train to Santiago de Cuba takes from 15 to 18 hours to reach its final destination.

Trains to the central and western regions of Cuba depart from the "Estación Tulipán", Nuevo Vedado, Calle Tulipán.

Trains to the district of Casablanca and to Matanzas depart from the "Estación Ferroviaria de Casablanca".

Air Travel → Travel in Cuba

Addresses and Stone Markers

Orientation in Havana is for some visitors not all that easy. An example will illustrate how an address is to be read: *Hotel Deauville,* Avenida Italia No. 1, entre Malecón y San Lázaro, Centro Habana, is to say: the hotel is in the Centro Habana district on Avenida Italia bordered by Malecón and Calle San Lázaro.

The situation is similar in Vedado. The streets in this district have no names but only numbers or letters. These are not on the houses themselves or on any signs but on stone markers at the intersections. One address as an example: Calle 3 No. 1015, entre 10 y R is to be read as follows: the house number 1015 is on Calle 3 in the block bordered by Calle 10 and Calle R. And: some streets are only known by their popular name. The lower segment of Calle 23 is merely called "La Rampa". Calle 9 is known to most of the residents only as "La Línea", Calle G is simultaneously known as "Avenida de los Presidentes", and Calle 7 is also referred to as "Calzada".

History

The date when the first human settlements on Cuba evolved around ten thousand years ago. At that time the first Indian settlers came to the island from Venezuela and penetrated the new land from the east to the western extremities. When Columbus "discovered" Cuba three Indian peoples differing in language and cultures populated this island. The Guanahatabeyes in the western regions of Cuba were not as highly developed as the Siboneys in Central Cuba and the Tainos to the east. These tribes were familiar with all of the methods of securing food: they hunted, collected fruits, farmed the land and fished the waters. Only the women wore a type of clothing: a loin cloth. Their status in the society was highly regarded since they played a decisive role in the food supply by collecting forest fruits and roots.

Rodrigo de Xerxes, sent as a scout by Columbus was the first European to see these smoking Indians and described them as "chimney men". Since this time, the rolled plant smoked by the Indians made its way into the European salons and became known as the cigar.

When Columbus landed with three caravels near what is now the city of →*Gibara* on October 28, 1492, around 300,000 Indians lived on the island. Contact with the populace was peaceful and Columbus thought he had reached the goal of his dreams, namely finding the sea route to India. His error remained unknown to him during his lifetime.

In 1511, the systematic conquest of Cuba began which resulted in the systematic eradication of the native population. The priest Bartolomé de las Casas, who served in the conquest of Cuba in the army under Diego Velázquez (later the first Spanish governor) reported these events in his "Brief Report on the devastation of West Indian lands".

The first seven cities in Cuba were founded: →*Baracoa*, →*Santiago de Cuba*, →*Bayamo*, Puerto Principe (later: →*Camagüey*), →*Trinidad*, →*Sanctí Spiritus* and La Habana. The Indians who survived the barbary of the first military campaigns became slaves, the private property of nobility and clergy. In turn the Indians were driven into the gold mines where they died en masse through brutality, inhumane working conditions and illnesses to which they had not yet built up immunity. Around the middle of the 16th century, the native Indian population had ceased to exist, marking the beginning of importing slaves from Africa.

The gold on Cuba was sparse and quickly exhausted. For this reason many Spaniards lost any further interest in Cuba and moved on to Mexico, following rumours of vast and unimaginable gold treasures. Those who did stay, took up raising livestock and agriculture.

The port city of Havana did, however, develop into the most important intermediate station for soldiers and soldiers of fortune on their way to the legendary "El Dorado". The famed silver fleet "La Flota" received a military escort here for its return trip to Spain, a desperate necessity considering the fact that the Caribbean was swarming with European pirates. These pirates also pillaged the coastal towns so often that many demoralised residents resigned and moved inland to found cities at a safe distance from the sea. However, mighty fortresses also resulted, built along the entrance to the bays; almost every larger town on the coast has such a relic from this swashbuckling period. However, the pirates were not only a thorn in Cuba's side, they also contributed to the economic growth of this colony. In fact they systematically broke the Spanish monopoly on trade and not only attacked settlers but also supplied them with coveted commodities and luxury articles from Europe, they strengthened the autonomy of the Creoles, the descendants of the Spaniards born in Cuba and helped the cities flourish economically. Just about everyone played a role in the smuggling trade from bishops to the slaves, and quite often took place with the silent consent of the governor.

During the 17th century, sugar became the new "magic word". Large land owners planted extensive fields of sugar cane – a luxury good so valuable it was sold by the gram in Europe.The huge sugar ane plantations were worked by armies of African slaves. However, as long as the Spanish trade monopoly, as fragile as it was, still existed it hindered the free development of the economy and with this, the production of sugar as well. Of the main export goods tobacco, pelts and sugar only enough was produced to satisfy the demand back in Europe.

A rebellion of the plantation owners and the tobacco farmers at the beginning of the 18th century was bloodily quashed by the Spaniards. Instead of keeping with the times and giving up the trade monopoly, they opened the monopoly to the wealthiest Creole merchants and this brought a system into the process of underdevelopment. The monopolists usually sold consumer goods at ten times the purchase price in order to use the profits to get into sugar production. A fantastically wealthy upper class resulted – the "Sacchariocracy" which exploited the overwhelming majority of the population, small farmers and slaves without scruple. The colony's affluence was soon exclusively dependent on sugar. Other branches of the economy were completely neglected, making it necessary to import food after only a short time. Meanwhile, the sugar cane depleted the nutrients in the soil. Huge areas were left ecologically devastated, a legacy with which Cuba still has problems today.

However, compared to Jamaica, Haiti and Barbados the sugar giants of that time, Cuba's sugar production was relatively humble. The two decisive events which led to a change in the situation came from the outside. After many unsuccessful attempts England was finally able to conquer Havana in 1762. Eleven months later they did clear out of the city in exchange for Florida; this short period was, however, sufficient to dissolve the Spanish monopoly and bring as many more slaves to the country as the Spaniards had during the former fifteen years. After the English withdrew, the Spanish began where they had left off. Trade and commerce had liberalised and Cuba geared up to the sugar export as dictated by the foreign demand.

Simultaneously, Cuba profited from the slave uprising on the neighbouring island of Haiti where 450,000 slaves drove 40,000 of their tormentors from the island. This meant the end of Cuba's main competition in sugar production. At the beginning of the 19th century, Cuba ultimately became the leader on the sugar market. More sugar of course meant more slaves. The number of African slaves working the plantations rose from 30,000 in 1762 to ten times that only ten years later. In 1817 there were more blacks than whites at times. Exactly how many Africans were taken to Cuba during the colonial period remains unknown. Many died during the ships crossings. The rash development of sugar production had brought dramatic consequences for Cuba

economically, ecologically and politically. The social inequality was immense, the food supply for the poorer population was catastrophic due to the mono-culture and the fertility of the soil decreased drastically. While Cuba followed the other islands in the Antilles on their way to economic independence, Cuba itself followed a political development unique in all of Latin America. As the only remaining Spanish colony, Cuba held on tight to the apronstrings of its greedy mother Spain. The plantation owner with slaves often thought of breaking away from Madrid; however the trauma of Haiti and the thought of having a fate similar to the French plantation owners on the neighbouring island ultimately kept the upper class under the protective auspices of Spain.

And it also came to uprisings which did not remain confined to the region; however, all were brought under control by force. It was only when the discontent peaked because the social classes which were smuggling to secure their existence but needed not fear the oppositional slaves joined forces with the opposition that the situation became critical to Madrid. How-ever, common military attacks on the Spaniards did not yet occur. The political goals of the Cubans were still too diverse. It was the wealthy lawyer and plantation owner Carlos Manuel de Céspedes who first recognised that the question of nationality could not be solved without considering the social problems. On October 10, 1868, he freed the slaves working on his plantation, proclaimed the free republic of Cuba and declared war on Spain. Members of all races and social classes joined the Mambises (freedom fighters). Among them, equality of races pervaded for the first time in Cuban history. The first war of independence lasted ten years and was fought with embittered dedication. The Spanish army could find no appropriate means to combat the guerrilla warfare and their control over Cuba receded to the cities along the main trade routes while the rural areas were under the control of the Mam-bises. Ultimately, both parties were exhausted, without a decisive victory for either side. A compromise was reached in 1878. The freedom fighters opted to forego national independence in favour of general amnesty, the guarantee of civil rights for all Cubans and the abolishment of slavery.

A weak compromise as time would tell because Madrid retracted these reforms anyway, reinstated slavery and had critics imprisoned. Shortly there-after, an economic crisis shook the already unstable country since the tobacco, coffee and sugar crops were almost completely destroyed by the war. The competition of beet sugar from Europe, caused the price on the world market for cane sugar to plummet. In order to make Cuban sugar able to

The construction of the "Castillo del Morro" fortress was the answer to continuous pillaging by pirates

compete again, the entire sugar production would have to be modernised and employ wage workers instead of slaves. Spain, however, failed to recognise the signs of the times and thus the United States intervened. Huge sums were invested in sugar production and soon the United States bought and sold a multiple of that which Spain did in Cuba. Spain's reaction was a large tax increase in order to take its part of the new affluence; Washington reacted with a stop on all sugar imports from Cuba. In this ticklish economic situation, the second war of independence (1895-1898) broke out. This was the last anti-colonial war in Latin America and standing at the front of the troops this time was José Martí (1853-1895) who is still honoured as the forerunner of independence. Untiringly, Martí gained support to free Cuba while in exile and collected a horde of Cuban patriots. Their demands were: agricultural reform, educational reform, emancipation of women, equality of races and the complete national independence. At the same time Martí called for a return to the traditional roots. Martí was also one of the few to recognise the danger of the US influence for the sovereignty of his country. However, his companions, among others the Generals Antonio Maceo and Máximo Gómez, from the first war of independence were less visionary politicians and more for strategic actions, and thus Martí's words of caution went unheeded.

Martí already fell in one of the first battles near Dos Ríos – an incomparable loss (→Bayamo).

The war lasted another three years and embittered battles were fought. Spain dispatched 240,000 soldiers to defend its last colony in America; however, the Mambises would ultimately secure the military victory. Martí had appraised the United States desire for power quite correctly. After the battleship "Maine" was sent under the pretext of protecting United States property and interests and exploded in the harbour of Havana for unknown reasons, 18,000 marines were sent to Cuba and defeated the already retreating Spanish army and were greeted by the Mambises as liberators.

The rude awakening would follow shortly: the North Americans occupied Santiago de Cuba and Havana, completely ignored the armed revolutionary government and took up negotiations with Spain.

The first military intervention (which would be followed by more) lasted up to 1902. Meanwhile the sugar barons, the tobacco industry and the wealthy merchants banded together with US capital used to purchase huge plots of land and quickly increased its influence. The both famous and infamous "Platt Amendment" was adopted into the new constitution in 1901, empowering the "big brother" to the north to intervene militarily at any time as long as" the liberty of the Cuban people" was deemed to be in jeopardy – in reality, nothing more than a blank cheque, with which Washington could do as they please on the Caribbean island. On May 20, 1902 Cuba received **independence.**

The period to follow is called the period of the pseudo-republic by historians today. The North American ambassador in Havana was the unseen power behind the Cuban president and the United States Embassy, the actual power centre. In domestic policy, a climate of corruption and oppression pervaded. North American companies now exclusively dominated the Cuban economy. Thirteen US sugar factories, for example, owned 47% of the land area set aside for sugar cane crops, 90% of the nickel, iron, copper, manganese and chrome mines were under North American ownership as part of the strategic reserve of the United States. Moreover, the US controlled the entire energy supply as well as the telecommunications network.

With the exception of sugar, Cuba itself produced very little; therefore, the country was forced to import everything. For the bourgeois "sugar-class", entire meals were flown in from Paris, while farm workers had little or nothing to eat. The "American way of life" changed the Cuban lifestyle drastically; US capital and the mafia transformed Havana to a glittering playground and brothel for the North.

All the while, the rural infrastructure remained underdeveloped. The monies designated for these regions seldom got any further than the city limits of Havana. Medical attention for the farming population was catastrophic. Children were undernourished and plagued by parasites. If any medications were imported at all along with the luxury articles, then they never reached the rural population. Only every third child went to school. The average life expectancy was 55 years of age and those who fled this misery to Havana mostly landed in the orange crate shacks in the slum districts.

During the First World War, the island experienced an unprecedented boom due to the inflated sugar prices. This affluence, was, however, to end abruptly; the sugar prices dropped to all time lows and the entire economy was shaken to the core. With this crisis – as was already the case before – the social tension reached the boiling point. Workers and farmers got involved in riots with the police and US troops had to repeatedly protect the government from its own citizens.

The dictatorship of Gerardo Machado, the "butcher" began in 1924. Antonio Mella, the leader of the Communist party founded in 1925 was murdered, the discontent population was held in check through the fear and terror of the "Porra", Machado's special troops. In 1933, a general strike and pressure from the US ambassador ultimately led to Machado's resignation. Shortly thereafter, a young sergeant by the name of Fulgencio Batista took power after an army revolt. Batista, originally not on Washington's payroll, sought the complete national sovereignty of Cuba and consulted labour unions and student associations in this goal. When Washington dispatched four battleships and the entire Atlantic fleet to Cuba to intimidate the apparently undesirable new ruler, Havana was to experience an unprecedented mass demonstration. For this reason, the United States troops would ultimately forego landing and instead took up negotiation with Batista personally. Young and ambitious, he soon complied with North American interests and subsequently the "Platt Amendment" was revoked as a compromise.

During the Second World War, the sugar industry experienced renewed prosperity. The warring nations also wanted to be supplied with meat. Tenant farmers and small farmers were driven from their land in order to create pastureland for livestock. In 1944, Batista was forced to resign because he had not taken the reaction of the enraged farmers into account. However, corruption and nepotism became increasingly worse in the governments to follow, civil rights were reduced, the labour market was repressed and the leader of the sugar workers was shot in public. Desperation and hopelessness were so extreme that most of the citizens considered it liberation when Batista secured power once again through a coup supported by the military leaders and the US. This time he meant business: the congress and all political parties were dissolved and the dictatorship was pure and simple a dictatorship with no concessions. The dissatisfaction quickly swept through large portions of

Magnificent, old villas - reminiscent of the colonial times

the population, the church and even the army. In January 1953, it came to bloody conflicts between students and the police. On July 26, patriots attempted to storm the Moncada military base in Santiago de Cuba under the leadership of a young lawyer by the name of Fidel Castro *(→also Granjita Siboney),* the attack failed and many rebels lost their lives. The speech in defense of the rebels by the then 27 year old Castro before the military court was destined to become world famous. In it Castro mercilessly counters the dictatorship, provides a firm basis for the rights of the oppressed populace to armed resistance and details the concrete concepts for a new social system. He closed with the words "As for me, I know, that prison will be harsh as it has never been for anyone before, full of threats, full of mean and cowardly rage, but do not fear it as I do not fear the rage of the miserable tyrants who killed seventy of my brothers. Sentence me, it doesn't matter, the course of history will be my acquittal".

After spending a year and a half in prison on the then Isla de los Pinos (Isla de la Juventud today) he was freed under pressure from the public. He went into exile in Mexico. Here he met the Argentinian physician and revolutionary Ernesto "Che" Guevara. With him and other Cuban patriots he prepared for his return to Cuba.

On Decmber 2, 1956 everything was ready: with 80 men on board, the "Granma" yacht landed near the village of Belic, south of Niquero in the Oriente region. The revolutionaries were not to succeed, their arrival was divulged and only twelve of Batista's soldiers could survive the hailstorm of bullets, among them Fidel Castro and his brother Rául, "Che" Guevara, Camilo Cienfuegos and Universo Sanchez. They split up and retreated to then meet in the wilderness of the Sierra Maestra to plan the armed resistance. It didn't take long before they had won the support of the farmers. Many came to "Che" for medical attention, they sent their children to learn to read and write from the rebels. In July 1958, the rebels numbered 3,000.

At first, Batista did not take the rebels in the distant Sierra Mestra seriously. It was first when the opposition took the initiative in the cities after the failed "Student Revolutionary Directorate" attack on the presidential palace that he struck back. In Spring 1958, Batista's troops set out with aircrafts and tanks on a large scale attack in the Sierra Maestra; which, however, was warded off after 70 days. The rebels continually grew in numbers. An election called by Batista, now under pressure, on November 3, 1958 was boycotted by 80% of the voting population. Toward the end of the same year the rebels ultimately took Sanctí Spiritus, Santa Clara and Santiago de Cuba. On New Year's Eve of 1958, the hated dictator fled the island with his family and leading members of the government. Fidél Castro and his army had succeeded. They arrived in Havana on January 8, 1959.

On May 21, 1959 Fidél Castro defined the character of the Cuban Revolution as follows: "Capitalism sells out humanity, communism, with its totalitarian concepts sacrifices civil rights... we do not condone the one or the other... Our revolution is neither red nor olive green. It is clothed in the colour of the rebel army from the Sierra Maestra."

At first, the United States and its Cuban collaborators believed they could quickly bring the new rulers under control. However, the new government meant business with the revolution: it dissolved the congress, fired 50% of all civil servants and condemned 500 of the former Batista's supporters to death. Drastic price decreases in the social sector (rents, electricity and medication) were undertaken as well as a reform of the social security system and a general wage increase. However, serious problems both within the country and outside first arose with the agricultural reform of May 17, 1959. Every tract of land over 400 hectares (1,000 acres) was seized and this hit many US property owners. The climate between Havana and Washington quickly worsened. Simultaneously, an uprising of counterrevolutionaries began in the Sierra del Escambray.

What would follow was an open fight. During this time, Cuba used its new economic orientation against the United States. On the one hand Cuba secured new trade partners like the USSR and the People's Republic of China; on the other, the conflict with the United States came to a head. The United States reacted to the nationalisation by the Cuban government by revoking the sugar quotas and ultimately with an embargo. When Washington declared a trade embargo with Cuba on October 19, 1960 and the socialist character of a revolution was officially declared, thousands of affluent Cubans fled the island, among them doctors, technicians and specialised labourers. In 1961 Havana began a campaign against illiteracy to counter the lack of specialised labourers in the long run. Within only one year, the illiteracy index could be decreased from 23.6% to 3.9%. At the beginning of 1961, the United States broke off diplomatic relations with Cuba. The Pentagon and the CIA prepared for military intervention. April 17, 1961 marked the invasion by a brigade of exiled Cubans trained in the United States in the →*Bay of Pigs*. After 72 hours of fighting, they were forced to retreat, the invasion remained unsuccessful.

Resulting from this defeat, Washington reacted with a comprehensive trade embargo, which had horrific effects on the Cuban economy which was geared to the American presence after decades of trade. Cuba's economy was – once more – on the edge of collapse. Simultaneously, Washington prepared another invasion on Cuba, this time openly. Cuba won the support of the other world power, the Soviet Union. At the end of 1962, the United States began a massive manoeuvre off the coast of Puerto Rico and Cuba. The US justified this action by the fact that satellite pictures revealed the presence of Soviet missile bases on Cuba. It was first when President Kennedy promised the UN that no invasion would take place – this on October 27 – that the Soviet Union did dismantle their missile launching ramps. The "Cuban Crisis" was over indeed (for the time being) and the US had accomplished nothing – except an ever-increasing radicalisation of the revolutionary government.

The battle for an economy with a solid foundation, however, proved much more difficult. Attempts to break the dependency on the sugar monoculture by producing cotton, soybeans and rice would fail. Concepts were sought through a long public discussion which came to be known as the "Planning Debate".

At first, a group demanding central planning and management could establish itself. However, the result was negative. The old rebels from the Sierra Maestra had to accept the fact that moral incentives like solidarity, collective responsibility and the overcoming of egoism, were not sufficient to change the mentality of the populace overnight. The factors worked inefficently. For this reason, the motto became "Each to his own ability, each to his own productivity" since 1970. Extra work was rewarded with a bonus and the workforce was increasingly included in managerial decisions.

As early as the mid 1960s, a *Second Agricultural Reform* transferred ownership of all tracts of land over 67 hectares (167.5 acres) to the state. This was a lethal blow to large land owners.

The expansion of the economy failed. One was forced to come to the painful conclusion that Cuba would remain dependent on the export of sugar. The government then changed its strategy. Why not make the monoculture the motor of Cuba's development? Where else would the desperately needed agricultural machinery and the expansion of the fishing fleet come from.

In 1965, the *PURS* (PURS = Partido Unificado de la Revolucion Socialista, Unified Party of the Socialist Revolution) was changed to *PCC* (PCC = Partido Communista de Cuba, the Communist Party of Cuba). Dr. Fidél Castro was named Chairman.

In 1968, all trade and service businesses were nationalised, since the black market threatened to get completely out of control. In 1972, Cuba became a member of the COMECON (Council for Mutual Economic Assistance). The subsequent years continued to be characterised by decentralisation and democratisation of production and decision processes. The living standard of the population rose.

Cuba has experienced a diplomatic "thaw" since the mid 1970s. Diplomatic relations with a number of western countries were re-established. The United States allowed the members of the OAS (Organisation of American States) to redefine their relations to Cuba. Foreign US companies no longer needed to adhere to the embargo a development apparent even to the tourists whose

Coca-Cola now came from Panama. Cuba's educational system meanwhile "produced" so many doctors, teachers and scientists that the country was able to send trained professionals (but also soldiers) to Angola and Mozambique.

Under President Carter, tourism from the United States was abruptly boosted. In 1979, Havana hosted the so-called "block-free", among which Cuba also counted. The revolution had brought every Cuban modest affluence or at least a humane existence.

However, in 1980, the government was to experience a trauma: over 130,000 Cubans, most of which belonged to the post-revolution generation, occupied the Peruvian Embassy in Havana, demanding the right to emigrate to the United States. Castro announced that a Revolution could not be undertaken with these type of people. He had their departure arranged via the Mariel Harbour.

As the "freedom fleet" departed from Miami, over a million people demonstrated their solidarity with the Revolution in the streets of Havana. After that, tough repatriation negotiations between the two nations took place; many of the expatriate Cubans were disappointed with the land of "unlimited opportunity".

Granjita Siboney: the siege on the Mocada Fortress was planned here in 1953

Despite this the government in Havana faced an uncertain future. An agreement with the United States from 1984 concerning the reuniting of families and an insured departure quota of 20,000 Cubans annually had meanwhile been revoked by the Cuban government. The dissatisfaction, especially among young people in regard to the scarcity of consumer goods, the modest standard of living and the limitations on travel became apparent. What massive military and political threats were not able to accomplish, seemed to be achieved by the US media through its radio and television programmes which brought information of the political upheavals in eastern Europe and the Soviet Union into the Cuban households. The position of the Cuban government which continued to propagate Castro's maxim "socialism or death" became increasingly difficult. The revolutionary slant of the Cuban decreased not only because of the renewed scarcity in supply. It would become the goal for the future to enthuse young people in Cuba for the construction of a new society, which had by no means been completed. This would prove to be a difficult task for the meanwhile old freedom fighters led by Fidél Castro, who out of principle would not join the Soviet Union and their former allied socialist nations in their new cause.

Holguín

The city of Holguín was founded in 1523 and named after a Spanish captain. It is situated in the middle of an extensive, fertile cattle-breeding region. Before the arrival of the Spaniards this region was already densely populated with Taino Indians. One of their settlements was named "Cubanacán" and once stood on the same site as the present-day city of Holguín. Cuba's name was derived from this former settlement. Today, Holguín is home to a population of 180,000, the main sectors of the economy are breeding livestock and sugar cane crops.

Holguín / **Sights**

Museo de Historia, Central Square. This exhibition documents the significance of the Holguín Province during the wars of independence *(→History)*. In 1868 Calixto Garcia, a famous general allied with the freedom fighters besieged the building since Spanish governmental troops barricaded themselves here. The museum is open Monday to Saturday from noon to 7:30 pm.

Museo de Historia Natural Carlos de la Torre. Calle Maceo No. 129, corner of Martí y Luz Caballero. The Museum of Natural History houses over 4,000 snail shells. It is open Tuesday to Saturday from 8 am to noon and 1 to 5 pm; Sundays from 8 am to noon.

La Loma de la Cruz, the hill of the cross is a popular site of pilgrimage from days long since past. An outdoor stairway leads up over 150 steps to the top of the hill where a cross has stood since 1790.

Casa de la Trova, Central Square. Local music groups perform music here, typical of this region. Directly next to it is the **Casa de la Cultura** with changing painting exhibits and a graphic studio. Closed Mondays.

Holguín / **Practical Information**

Accommodation

Hotel *Pernik,* Avenida Anniversario y Plaza de la Revolución. A modern tourist hotel in the centre of town. Double rooms from $34 (£20).

Hotel *Turquino,* in the centre of town; simple and inexpensive. Double rooms from around $20 (£12).

Motel *El Bosque,* Carretera Mayarí, Reparto Nuevo Holguín. Double rooms from around $23 (£14).

Motel *Mirador de Mayabe,* near the city in Parque Mayabe. Offering a beautiful view of the nature reserve in the Mayabe Valley. Double rooms from $20 (£12).

Restaurants

All of the hotels also have good restaurants. Especially worth recommending is the restaurant in the Motel *Mirador de Mayabe.*

Holiday Apartments →*Accommodation*

Holidays and Celebrations

Cuba took its history into its own hands in 1959. Legal holidays and national patriotic holidays are just as directly related to the independence of the country as the names of the streets, squares, schools and hospitals. Work continues as normal on Christian holidays like Christmas and Easter, while on legal holidays all banks, shops and many museums remain closed. This is not the case on national commemorative holidays.

Legal Holidays

January 1: Diá de la Liberación (anniversary of the revolutionary victory in 1959).

January 2: Day of victory celebrations.

May 1: Labour Day.

July 26: Diá de la Rebledía Nacional (anniversary of the attack on the Moncada Base in Santiago).

National Commemorative Holidays

January 28: José Martí's birthday (the apostle of freedom).

February 24: anniversary of the beginning of the second war of independence.

March 8: Día de la Mujer (International Women's Day).

March 13: Anniversary of the student attack on the presidential palace in 1957.

July 30: Day of the Martyrs of the Revolution.

October 8: Anniversary of "Che" Guevara's death in Bolivia.

October 10: Día de la Cultura Cubana. The anniversary of the beginning of the first war of independence.

October 28: Day in Memory of Camilo Cienfuegos.

November 27: Anniversary of the assassination of eight medical students in the battle for liberty by the Spanish.

December 2: Anniversary of the landing of the "Granma" in Cuba.

December 7: Day in Memory of Antonio Maceo.

Events of Interest to Tourists

Second week in January: Tourists' Carneval in Varadero.

February 14: Valentines day is a large celebration in Cuba (many hotels are completely booked at this time.

In April: Festival of the Caribbean Culture in Santiago de Cuba.

Second Sunday in May: The Ernest Hemingway Fishing Competition in Barlovento, Havana.

In June: Festival des Cucalambé, rural folklore in Las Tunas.

From mid June to the first week in August: Carneval in Havana and Santiago de Cuba.

First week of December: Festival Nacional de Coros in Santiago de Cuba.

End of December: Parrandas von Remedios, Carneval parades.

In addition to these festivals taking place on a regular basis, there are numerous other events all over the island. Information on where exactly what is taking place is available through Cubatur *(Travel in Cuba/Cubatur and Intur).*

Hospitals →*Medical Care*

Hotels →*Accommodation*

Information → *Travel in Cuba/Cubatur and Intur;* →*Travel Documents*

La Guira National Park

La Guira National Park lies in the Sierra de los Organos in Cuba's western regions. Within its 22,000 square kilometres (8,580 square miles) it protects a piece of Cuba's ecological past: pine forests, cedar and mahogany trees are very dense like nowhere else on the island. The distance to *Havana* is 132 kilometres (83 miles).

Accommodation: *Saratoga* and *Libertad* in San Diego del Baños are two simple hotels, both priced from 15 Pesos.

Language

Cuba's official language is Spanish. Since, however, the Cubans are a rather unique mix of peoples with linguistic roots stemming from Indian, African and American languages and these are all reflected in the language spoken in Cuba, even the Spanish-speaking tourists will frequently have some difficulties. These can quickly be overcome by knowing that the Cubans simply do not pronounce some consonants. Among those consonants which are most commonly omitted are the *s,* the *t* and the *b.* It often seems very foreign when Cubans say the word *doctor;* it sounds like *doctol.* And this type of thing is true for a number of other words.

However, since the Cubans are very willing to help, seem to be very good at communicating through pantomime and – if all else fails – are also willing to slow their velocity of speech, one will get by quite well with Spanish throughout Cuba.

English can only be expected in the tourist centres where the large tour organisers have their tour guides based. These people are usually happy to help with linguistic difficulties.

Literature

The travel diaries of Christopher Columbus and Alexander von Humboldt are certainly worth reading as documents for a trip to Cuba. However, these are not light reading.

In addition to these are literary works by Hemingway like "The Old Man and the Sea" or political writings like José Martí's "With Quill and Machete".

One aid in the basics of speaking Spanish is also available from Hayit Publishing: "Hayit's Phrase Books: Spanish", published in 1993.

Maps

There are maps available at Cubatur offices around the world *(→Documents).* In Cuba maps are available in the Intur shops in the tourist hotels. However, there always seems to be a shortage of maps so if they are available it is a good idea to buy them straight away.

Mariel

The port city of Mariel on the Atlantic coast is famous throughout the world thanks to the "Freedom Fleet" which departed from here for Florida with ten thousand Cubans wanting to leave the country in 1980. Founded in 1762, this city has an electrical plant, the largest cement factory in Cuba and a factory for the processing of sisal. It lies 48 kilometres (30 miles) west of Havana.

Markets

In numerous cities and towns, there are markets with unrestricted sales ("Venta Libre") which are good places to stock up on bread and fresh fruit, depending on what is available at the time.

Matanzas

Situated only 38 kilometres (24 miles) west of the tourist centre of Varadero, Matanzas is still a very good town to experience the Cuban everyday. The city was founded in 1690 and is home to a population of over 100,000 today. It is the most important port for sugar export on Cuba's northern coast. During the 19th century it even achieved the status of sugar capital of Cuba because over half the sugar designated for export was produced in the regions surrounding Matanzas. During the sugar boom, Matanzas developed a veritable "salon culture": the sugar barons and wealthy citizens caused art and culture to flourish and made Matanzas into Cuba's Athens.

Matanzas / **Sights**

La Vina, corner of Santa Teresa and Calle Milanés near the Pharmaceutical Museum. Restored with a love for detail, this is a typical Cuban grocery shop from the 19th century.

Teátro Sauto, Plaza de la Vigia on the Matanzas Bay. Probably the most significant building from the Cuban neoclassicistic period. Constructed in 1863, it later fell into a state of decay, only to be restored after the revolution.

Castillo de San Severino, Avenida del Muelle on the harbour north of the city. This fortress is the oldest structure in Matanzas and dates back to the era of pirate attacks.

Bellamar Caves, Finca la Alcancia. The network of caves approximately 2 kilometres (1 mile) in length was discovered in 1850 quite by chance. In these caves are underground rivers, stalagmites and small "cathedral" of stalactites. The caves are around 2 kilometres (1 mile) outside the city.

caves are underground rivers, stalagmites and small "cathedral" of stalactites. The caves are around 2 kilometres (1 mile) outside the city.

The tourist offices in the hotels organise tours to these caves. The caves are open to the public daily from 9 am to 4:30 pm.

Museo Farmaceutico, Calle Milanés No. 4951, corner of Ayuntamiento. The Pharmaceutical Museum is unique in Cuba and all of Latin America. The chemist's shop (pharmacy) was set up in 1882 by a French man and operated by his family up to 1964. Worth seeing here are magnificent collections of old porcelain containers, pharmaceutical instruments, dried plants etc.

The Pharmaceutical Museum is open Monday to Saturday from 2 to 6 pm and 7 to 9 pm.

Medical Care

The Cuban health care system has become one of the best in Latin America, having been established in 1959. The hospitals are also equipped for more complicated operations. Havana has meanwhile become the destination for an intensive Latin American "health care tourism." This type of holiday can also be taken through Cubatur. The Medical care here is not namely only competent and exemplary but also much less expensive than anywhere else on the continent. Tourists from western industrialised nations pay the same low prices for medication as the Cubans. Furthermore the island has overcome its independence on imported medications. Eighty percent of all pills, drops and ointments are produced within the country itself. The first visit to a doctor, laboratory and stays in the hospital are all free.

Physicians can be reached easily both day and night from the hotels. Pharmacies are listed in the phonebook under the heading "farmacia". One can safely forego the malaria propholaxis which is obligatory for the other Central American countries. Cholera and Yellow Fever are also a thing of the past. Certificates of vaccination are only required to enter Cuba when coming from an infected area. However, be sure to be vaccinated for polio and tetanus before departureMedication that should be brought along is as follows: medication on repeat prescription, medication for diarrhoea, disinfectant for minor wounds as well as suntan lotion with a high protection factor. The latter is a must for any trip to Cuba since the Caribbean sun can cause severe sunburn.

Medication →*Medical Care*
Minas →*Camagüey/Excursions*

Music

Cuba seems to be fertile soil for producing musicians and poets, as the ethnologist Miguel Barnet once put it. Dances like the Chachachá, the Rumba and the Mambo gained success around the world originating in Cuba. Then it was the Salsa which was to sweep through western Europe and influence other musical styles. Most of the dance rhythms popular today trace their roots back to African slaves. The main musical instrument was the drum; later the plantation also gave them guitars, violins and trumpets first used in more refined social circles but then adapted to their own music as well. For festive occasions but also for everyday life, the Rumba was the most popular of the dances. This dance originates from the most diverse African tribes. Groups formed a circle from which individuals stepped inside the circle to dance. From this original form of Rumba, the erotic "Yambu" dance as well as the "Guaguanco" later developed. The original Rumba had nothing to do with the popular dance with the same name. Today, this original form is only performed during special occasions.

One musical style still popular today is the "Son". It can be recognised by an interplay of soloist and choir, in which the frequent repetition of the refrain and the polyrhythms show strong African influence. Popular instruments used in the "soneros" are the guitar, wooden blocks called "claves" and drums called "congas". The "son" has greatly influenced the music performed by present-day groups like "Irakere", "Grupo Afro-Cuba", "Sierra Maestra", "Los Van-Van", and "Rumbavana".

The "Nueva Trova" was the musical answer to the changes in the politics and society in the 1960s. The new Cuban song received its most significant impulses from the protest movements in North America and Europe. The most widely known proponents of this musical movement include Silvio Rodriguez, Pablo Milanés, Sergio Vitier, Eduardo Ramos, and Sara González.

Nudism

Bathing nude or topless is not allowed in Cuba. One should observe this strictly. If it is necessary to change on the beach, do so discretely.

Nuevitas →*Camagüey/Excursions*

The People of Cuba

Cuba has a total population of 10. 5 million. The population growth could be reduced to 0.9%, an unusually low rate for Latin America. The average life expectancy is 77 years of age compared to 55 before the revolution.

The profile of the population is characterised by young people. Around 53% of the Cubans over 15 years of age are employed and 97% of children between 6 and 12 attend school.

Compared to other islands in the Antilles, Cuba is less densely populated; however, the proportion of the urban population is high at 60%. The most dense population area is the greater Havana region, in which 20% of Cuba's population lives.

The capital is home to over two million residents and is also the largest city in Cuba, followed by Santiago de Cuba (population: 370,000), Camagüey (population: 245,000) and Holguín (population: 180,000). It is worth mentioning here that Havana, as the only city in Latin America, has not grown disproportionately thanks to the decentralisation policy implemented by the revolutionary government. Thus, it has been spared the fate of other massive metropolises like Mexico City and Rio de Janeiro.

Chief of State Castro attempted to solve the problem with racial discrimination through equal rights legislation. It was Castro who made the observation that all Cubans had African blood in their veins. Since 1971, there have been no more census questions regarding the ethnic background of the population. At that time, half of Cuba's population were descendants of European, mostly Spanish, immigrants. The other half comprised about equal proportions of blacks and mullatos.

As is the case with the other islands in the Antilles, the native Indian population had been completely wiped out by the Spaniards after only 50 years. Cuban ethnologists have, however, discovered a handful of small villages in the eastern most regions of the island, the residents of which still practice precolumbian burial rituals.

Finally, the descendants of Chinese workers, who were brought to Cuba after slavery was abolished, account for 1% of the population. They live predominantly in Havana.

Photography

As is the case everywhere in the world, one should be tactful when taking pictures of people and ask their permission in advance. Generally, the Cubans have nothing against having their picture taken.

Santiago's Carnival is more colourful and lively than that of Havana: streets transform into a witch's caldron churning with activity

Photography supplies like film, flash cubes and batteries should be brought along in sufficient quantities since they cannot be found everywhere in Cuba. If they are available, then they are usually much more expensive.

The old East German x-ray machines at the airports are said to damage film. For this reason, take film in a clear plastic bag in a carry on and have it hand checked at customs clearance.

The rays of the sun are very intense along the coast. Film with a medium light sensitivity are therefore the best suited for these conditions. For the nightly shows, one should choose a higher speed of film and use a flash.

Military bases may not be photographed; one must always ask permission before taking pictures in museums or photographing industrial or agricultural facilities.

Pinar del Río

Pinar del Río was founded in 1571 and was first named Nueva Filipana. Before the city could be founded, the native Guanahatabeyes population of this area who lived as hunters and gatherers were first eradicated. After "sleeping" for over two hundred uneventful years, the tobacco farmers in this remote city were able to go around the Spanish monopoly on trade. During the time to follow, they were able to establish a self-confident and independent social class. Today Pinar del Río has a population of around 120,000 and is the capital of the province. Ornate, neoclassicistic buildings characterise the inner city. The distance from Havana is 175 kilometres (110 miles).

Pinar del Río / **Sights**

Téatro José Jácinto Milanés, Calle Martí corner of Colón. This theatre was dedicated in 1845 and can accommodate 500. It was a sign of prestige for wealthy citizens as well as being a focal point of cultural life in this city.

Museo Antonio Guiteras Holmes, Avenida Maceo No.202, corner of San Juan y O. Avenado. The history of the region and the role of the city during the battle against the British dictatorship are documented in this museum.

Museo de Ciencias Naturales, Calle Martí No. 202 corner of Avenida Commandante Pináres. The museum is housed in an architectural curiosity: a building with an adventuresome mixture of every possible type of architecture. The museum is open Tuesday to Sunday from 2 to 11 pm.

Museo de Tabáco (Fabric de Tabáco), housed in the former "Antigua Cárcel" prison. The blue inconspicuous building is difficult to find; it is best to ask around – everyone will know where it is. The Museum's theme is the production of cigars.

Guayabita Rum Factory, in the centre of town. This is where the "guayabita del pinar" rum is produced; a type of liqueur which is very popular with the Cubans and only available in Pinar del Río.

Casa de la Cultura, Calle Máximo Gómez No.108, across from the Palace of Justice. Cultural events take place here every evening.

Casa de la Trova, Calle Velez Caviedes, corner of Yagruma y Retiro. Concerts by local Argentinean and Mexican groups frequently take place here.

Sightseeing Tour Pinar del Río – Viñales. A bus tour including a meal, a tour through the tobacco and rum factory for $30 (£18) (→*Office for Individual Tourism*).

Pinar del Rio / **Practical Information**

Accommodation

Hotel *Pinar del Río,* Calle Martí Autopista, Tel: 50-7179. Doubles start at $27 (£16). All rooms have a bathroom and toilet, air conditioning, radio, telephone and a balcony. Restaurant, bar, cafeteria, discotheque, swimming pool and Intur shop. Tourist Information office.

Hotel *Vuelta Abajo,* Calle Martí No. 101, entre San Juan y Cuarteles, Tel: 2303. Double rooms are priced around $30 (£18). All rooms with a bathroom and toilet, air conditioning and radio. Restaurant, bar and discotheque.

On Calle Martí or nearby are also several less expensive hotels.

Hotel *La Marina,* Calle Martí, entre Morales y Avenado.

Hotel *Moderna,* Calle Avenado, entre Martí y Gómez.

Hotel *Globo,* Calle Martí, entre Medina y Isabel Rubio.

Recently, several new hotels have been built on the outskirts of the city.

Camping: *Aguas Claras,* around 8 kilometres (5 miles) toward Viñales on the right-hand side. Small bungalows, the camping area has a pool, bar and restaurant; $14 (£9).

Excursions

Cayo Levisa, a small wooded island off the atlantic coast. The tourist offices in the hotels in Pinar del Río organise swimming and fishing trips there. The catch is usually lobster and prawns which are then prepared on the beach as a meal.

Restaurants

Restaurant *La Casona,* Calle Martí corner of Colón, open noon to 11 pm. Cuban cuisine in a Spanish colonial ambiance.

Restaurant-Cabaret *Rumayor,* one kilometre (1/2 mile) out of town on the road to Viñales. Many consider this the best restaurant in western Cuba. The speciality of this restaurant is "pollo ahumado" (smoked chicken) served with the "guayabita del pinar", a liqueur made from the guavas growing in this region.

Restaurant *La Taberna,* Calle Ramón Gonzales Coro No. 103, entre Solano Ramos y Retiro. Open noon to 11 pm and serving Spanish cuisine.

Restaurant *Mar Init,* Parque Independencia, a simple eating establishment.

Restaurant *Vuelta Abajo,* in the hotel with the same name on Calle Martí; Cuban cuisine.

Tourist Information

Cubatur, Calle Martí next to Hotel *Vuelta Abajo.* In addition to the standard services, this information office offers tours of the farms, the handicrafts workshops and an evening visit to the Cabaret-Restaurant Rumayor.

Transportation

Bus

"Terminal de Omnibus Interprovinciales" and "Terminal de Omnibus intermunicipales" are under one roof between Calle Colón and Com. Pinares.

Havana - Cuba's capital has a population of more than two million

The "interprovinciales" take passengers to Havana and Guane, the "intermunicipales" provide service to smaller towns in the surrounding regions (Ciudad Sandino, La Palma, Santa Lucía, →*Viñales,* Artemisa, Guane, La Bagada).
Collective Taxis
The old "maquinas" wait on the square in front of the bus terminal. A car to Havana costs 70 pesos.
Trains
The train station is at the end of Calle Com. Pinares. The trains operate between Havana and Guane.

Politics and Government

Since 1959, Cuba has been a socialist republic. The chief of state, chairman of the privy council and the head of the government is Fidél Castro Ruz. Simultaneously, he is also the chairman of the minister's council, general secretary of the Communist Party of Cuba and the commander-in-chief of the armed forces. Still, Cuban politics are not a one-man show. In 1976, the *Poder Popular* (the "people's power") was introduced following a referendum. This set a sign for the democratisation of the government and administration in Cuba. The Poder Popular is the focal point of political life. Candidates are nominated directly by the voters and not by the party or large political organisations. The candidates must regularly justify their political actions. If they fail, they are immediately voted out of office. Despite a basis of equality of the sexes, women are still clearly in the minority as political representatives. The communal representatives on the lowest level elect the delegates for the provincial council of the *Poder Popular* and they, in turn, elect delegates for the national council. Fifty percent of these delegates must also be communal representatives. This is to ensure that the contact to the people is maintained. The privy council answers to the national council and it, in turn, is answerable to the provincial council and so on. The national council appoints the supreme court, the revolutionary courts, the military courts and the people's tribunals. The latter are unique to Cuba because here, laymen – and not judicial experts – decide on cases of unsocial conduct.

Public Transport →*Travel in Cuba*

Religion

In Cuba, the church was always a church for the affluent. Baptisms and marriages were very expensive affairs and only Spaniards could become priests. Before the revolution, only ten percent of the population belonged to a church for this very reason. At present, 5% are members of Cuba's *Catholic Church.* The *Protestant Church* has 2% of the population backing it. In contrast to the Catholic Church, the Protestant Church has no qualms in working with the socialistic government and works hand in hand with it in creating the "new breed" of people.

Freedom of religion is set forth in the constitution of 1975. The government supports church activities in the areas of health care and care for the elderly. However, far more significant than a Christian profession of faith, are the *Afro-Cuban Religions,* once brought to the island by the African slaves and still tolerated today. The Yoruba and Conga Religion, the Santería and the Abakuá secret society are deeply rooted in the social mix which characterises Cuba. They have influenced the culture and have even absorbed the Christian religions. Their gods called *oríshas* are venerated through ceremonies and conjured up with all kinds of magical rituals of oracle priests. What is strange to see is the Afro-Cuban oríshas, revolutionary heroes and the Virgin Mary all next to each other on the altars of some priests. This association has led to a blurring of the religions: the Catholic saints all have an equivalent Afro-Cuban god – or vice versa.

"Santerías" or veneration ceremonies still take place today. During the final days of the Batista dictatorship it is reported that black priests and soothsayers were at their prime in the white upper class. Their social standing in the life of the individual has, however, noticeably changed. For many black as well as white Cubans, the Afro-Cuban sites and rituals have become similar to what the astrology columns in newspapers are to us.

Rental Cars →*Car Rental*
Restaurants →*Cuisine* and *individual entries*

Sancti Spíritus

As is the case for many coastal cities in Cuba, Sancti Spíritus is among the earliest established colonial bases on Cuba. It was founded in 1514 which means that it was also one of the first settlements in all of Latin America. Although situated deep inland, the city suffered greatly under pirate attacks during the 17th century.

Tobacco crops and livestock breeding brought the city's residents affluence and the old city district remains a beautiful example of Spanish architecture and culture even today. Meanwhile Sancti Spíritus is home to a population of 90,000 and is the capital of the Sancti Spíritus province. Dairy production, rice and vegetable crops supplement the city's economic base. The people in this region have been considered conservative for a long time; the new administrative and production methods introduced by the revolutionary government still meet with skepticism in this area.

Sancti Spiritus / **Practical Information**
Accommodation
Hotel *Zaza* (on the Presa Zaza Reservoir). Modern hotel directly at the largest reservoir in Cuba. Restaurant, bar, swimming pool, rental boats; double rooms from $27 (£16).
Restaurants
In Hotel *Zaza* (at the Presa Zaza Reservoir, only a few kilometres from Sancti Spiritus). There are also inexpensive snack bars surrounding the central square and the side-streets.
Sights
Worth seeing is the typical chess board layout of the city centre with the *Parish Church*. This church is among the oldest in Cuba and the best preserved. Its interior has a wonderful carved ceiling.
Museo de la Esclavitud, Parque Honorato, provides an overview of the history of slavery.

Santa Clara
The city of Santa Clara was founded in 1689 and has developed into a bustling industrial city. 170,000 residents live here, working in the largest textile mills in Cuba which were built with support from Japan as well as a cement factory, tobacco production and several sugar refineries in the region. The university in Santa Clara is one of the largest in the country. Toward the end of the Batista dictatorship, Santa Clara formed the backdrop for embittered battles between rebel units led by "Che" Guevara and government troops.

Sights: *Monumento al Tren Blindado,* near the entrance to the city toward Camajuani. This monument is made up of three armoured wagons intended to transport government soldiers into the occupied city. However the train was stopped by "Che's" soldiers which was ultimately decisive in the rebels' victory.

Santa Clara / **Practical Information**
Accommodation
Hotel *Santa Clara,* Parque Vidál. An old but well maintained hotel in the centre of town. Double rooms are priced from $20 (£12). During the month of December in 1958, this hotel was the last stronghold of the Batista troops. Bullet holes on the exterior of this building are a reminder of these "hot" days in December *(→History).*

Hotel *Central,* Parque Vidál. An inexpensive hotel with a restaurant and cafeteria.

Hotel *América,* Calle Mujica, entre Calle Maceo y Colón. An option when absolutely nothing else is available...

Motel *Los Caneyes,* Avenida Eucaliptos y Circunvalación. A holiday complex for tourists located outside the city. The bungalows are built after the pre-Columbian huts. Double rooms from $27 (£16).

Excursions

Modern rural workers' settlement *La Yaya.* This is a state operated farm which has specialised in livestock, run by former small farmers. The concept for this settlement was developed by Fidél Castro in 1970.

Hanabanilla Reservoir →Hanabanilla

Tobacco Factory

All three excursions are organised by *Cubatur* and can be booked in the office next to the *Santa Clara Libre.*

Restaurants

Restaurant *Santa Clara Libre,* in the hotel with the same name at Parque Vidál.

1878, Calle Máximo Gómez, entre Independencia y Martí. Cuban cuisine is served in a colonial atmosphere.

Casa del Queso, Calle Lorda, entre Independencia y Céspedes. Speciality of the house are cheeses, wine and ham.

Worth recommending is the inexpensive Cafeteria *Merendero el Soda* at Parque Vidál. Additional snack bars are located on Calle Martí between Calle Máximo Gomez and Villnendas.

Tourist Information

The *Cubatur* office is next to the *Santa Clara Libre* Hotel in Parque Vidál.

Transportation

Bus: Both bus terminals are on Calle Abreu. Reservations for buses to Santiago de Cuba and Havana must be made well in advance. The "intermunicipales" provide service to Sancti Spíritus, Cienfuegos, Cumanayagua, Coralillo, Sagrua and Remedios.

Train: In addition to trains to Havana and Santiago de Cuba, there is also a connection to Morón.

Santa Lucía

Santa Lucía is situated southwest of the canal leading from Nuevitas as the only access to the sea. Up until only a few years ago, the 20 kilometre (12 mile) sand beaches were still almost abandoned and clear, extending along the clear water. However, the speed of Cuba's development in terms of tourism becomes very apparent here: since the summer of 1990, Santa Lucía has become a popular destination for sun-worshippers and acquatic sports enthusiasts.

The city, however, offers little in the way of entertainment outside the hotel complexes. But this is the location of one of the largest coral reefs in the world, a fascinating underwater world for scuba divers. Here one can explore sunken ships, observe colourful tropical fish, experience gardens of black coral and the natural caves and tunnels. There are more than 15 diving areas to explore. It is most difficult here to obey the law against taking shells out of the country. Shells purchased at shops are only allowed to be brought out of the country by presenting a sales receipt.

It can become annoying if the wind blows from an unfavourable direction, bringing with it a plague of mosquitos. The so-called "jungle oil" can be of some help.

The beach is ploughed daily, removing the debris from the sea. The ocean flow falls off very gradually toward the reef and is covered with sea grass. Bathing sandals are recommended.

Because the management is still quite inexperienced overbooking at hotels is not uncommon.

Santa Lucía / **Practical Information**
Accommodation

Hotel *Tararaco,* right at the bus terminal and near the beach. A quiet and practically located complex with 62 beds. Rooms including breakfast cost $15 (£9), half board is possible, surcharge for a single room $15 (£9).

Hotel *Mayanabo,* around 50 yards from the beach, this generously laid out complex is in the middle category and has 450 beds. Friendly and helpful staff. Swimming pool, postal service, small supermarket. Very simple rooms with air conditioning and a separate bathroom. Rooms with breakfast start at $23 (£14), half and full board possible, single room surcharge is around $17 (£10).

Hotel *Villa Coral,* built in 1989, this is a large club complex in the middle category. Bungalows are equipped with air conditioning, bathroom, colour television, telephones and video channel. The staff is friendly and helpful; a doctor is available from 9 am to 5 pm. Restaurant, cafeteria, swimming pool, game centre, snack bar, two tennis courts, small supermarket, taxis, rental cars, tourism office. Rooms with breakfast start at $24 (£14), half and full board are possible, surcharge for single room around $17 (£10).

Activities

Sports

Equipment rental and lessons are availabe in the hotels.

Scuba Diving: theoretical and practical lessons at the coral reef. Around $80 (£47). Scuba diving tours: depending on the number participating, between $27 and $240 (£16 and £140).

Waterskiing: 15 minutes cost around $8 (£5).

Horse-drawn wagons: $1 (60p) per person.

Horseback Riding: Without a guide around $3 (£1.80), with guide $5 (£3).

Excursions

In the surrounding regions of Santa Lucía, there are no towns worth seeing. The state operated tourist organisation offers numerous excursions in conjunction with the hotels costing from $2 to $170 (£1.20 to £100). The tours to Havana and Santiago de Cuba (both including a show) last two days. In addition, there are tours to Trinidad, Holguín, Camagüey, Guardalavaca and the beaches of Los Cocos or Bonita. Furthermore, there are themed excursions like "sunset", "farmer's festival", "flamingos" and the like. Groups are usually from two to six persons and the excursions are highly recommended. At Hotel *Villa Coral* is a helicopter landing pad from which one can depart on lovely sightseeing flights. Destinations include Guardalavaca to visit the Dolphinarium (around $100/£60) or one can merely see Santa Lucía from the aerial perspective (around $25/£15for 15 minutes).

Restaurants

One place worth recommending is the grill in Hotel *Villa Coral* right next to the swimming pool. It serves lobster (around $12/£7) or filet steaks (around $4/£2.50), albeit only during lunchtime.

Las Bahamas, seafood restaurant directly on the beach around 2 kilometres (1 miles) from the hotel complexes.

Bon Say, on the access road between Hotel *Villa Coral* and Santa Lucía, around 500 yards from the hotel. Chinese food, the quality of which is however heavily dependent on the mood of the chef.

La Bocca Ferras, on the beach of Los Cocos, serving fish dishes.

Maternillo in the Hotel *Villa Coral* offers little variety but does have very good pizzas.

Transportation

Bus: The buses are in operation from 7 am to 11 pm, they are always overcrowded and do not depart according to any given schedule. Bus fare: 10 centavos.

Air Travel: The nearest airport is in Camagüey. The bus there takes around 1 hour.

Rental Cars: Ladas and Buggys are offered for around $25 to $30 (£15 to £18). Per week: $155 to $250 (£90 to £150), deposit $250 (£150). *Caution:* the roads are in very poor condition.

Taxi: base price $1 (60p) and 5¢ (3p) for each kilometre. For example: a taxi ride from a hotel to Camagüey with a tour of the city and then back to the hotel will cost around $60 (£35).

Santiago de Cuba

Santiago de Cuba was founded in 1514 and, as the capital of the Santiago de Cuba province, it is Cuba's "second capital city". All of Cuba's races and cultures flowed together here and every revolution Cuba was destined to experience began here.

Coloured Cubans determine the character of the city, making it the most Caribbean and liveliest city on the island. The population of 350,000 live by working at the harbour, the wharfs, a chemical plant set up after the revolution, factories for construction materials and a few copper mines in the nearby regions. Carnival in Santiago is celebrated more wildly than anywhere else.

Santiago de Cuba / **History**

Santiago quickly advanced to the most important city for commerce right after it was founded. The harbour became a base for the silver fleet and the largest proportion of the spoils from pillages in Mexico and Columbia were transported here. When Havana became the capital, Santiago turned to copper. The native Indian population had already extracted copper from the mountains in the region. The mines remained lucrative up into the 19th century and later African slaves initiated the first slave revolt on the island here.

The affluent Santiagueros only suffered under the unhealthy tropical heat in this bay area. Their houses built in the hills further inland did provide some escape from the relentless heat but were not protection from the pirate attacks. Pirates repeatedly penetrated deep into the bay, pillaged and burned the city. The fortress of "El Morro" built in 1642 at the entrance to the bay provided only limited protection because shortly thereafter the English arriving form Jamaica were able to conquer the city and burn it to the ground. The humiliated Santiagueros swore revenge and sent a fleet to the Bahamas only a short while later, killed a hundred English subjects and secured opulent spoils. When the English tried to found a colony east of the city 30 years later they were driven out by an embittered battle with the Santiagueros.

With the victory of the slave revolution in neighbouring Haiti *(→History);* 30,000 French farmers came to the greater Santiago region with their families at the end of the 18th century. They heavily influenced the city's lifestyle and economy. From this point on, Santiago experienced a golden age both economically and culturally. However, the trauma of a slave revolt as took place on the neighbouring island brought fear to the sugar and coffee plantation owners. The slaves were guarded more strictly in Santiago than anywhere else in Cuba. Farmers, farm workers and the liberal orientated population happily welcomed the first outbreak of the first war of independence. Antonio Maceo, a coloured son of the city brought his career all the way to General in the rebel army. During the time of the pseudo-republic (→*History*), Santiago de Cuba fell somewhat into insignificance.

Santiago de Cuba would only become a focal point after the unsuccessful storm of intellectuals on the Moncada military base. Considering the military's reign of terror, the populace backed the imprisoned survivors and were able to have their death penalties changed to long term prison sentences. After

Santa Lucía is a paradise for divers and snorkellers with fifteen enticing diving areas

1953, an underground city movement led by the Pais brothers formed. Later this movement supported the guerrilla warriors from the Sierra Maestra. The battle against the Batista dictatorship cost many Santiagueros their lives. It is that there was at least one death in every family at this time.

The dominance of the Batista troops was conclusively broken in December 1958. The populace prepared a triumphant reception for the victorious rebel army. On January 1, 1959, Fidél Castro officially declared the victory of the revolution from the city hall's balcony at the Céspedes Park.

Santiago de Cuba / **Sights**

Around the Parque de Céspedes:

The former City Hall: this can be easily recognised by its blue balconies. It was from one of these balconies that Fidél Castro announced the victory of the revolution to the cheering Santiagueros. Today, this is the seat of the Peoples Power *(→Politics and Government)*.

The Cathedral: The first church to stand on this site originates from 1528. However, earthquakes, pirate attacks and attacks by the English left it in a pitiable state, so that it was torn down at the end of the 18th century. The present-day cathedral was built on it's foundations. Only the choir stalls inside originate from the old church.

Casa de la Velázquez: The Casa de Velázquez lies on the western side of the park and is the oldest colonial building in Cuba. The first mayor of the city Hernán Cortéz had it built in 1522. On the ground floor, the gold from Indian tribes and the gold found in the surrounding areas was melted down. The first governor of the island Diego de Velázquez later moved into the upper floor. This building has housed the Museum of Colonial Art since 1971. On displays here are furnishings made from valuable woods and heavily padded travel trunks.

Hotel Casa Grande, across from *Casa de la Velázquez*. This is an impressive building built in the colonnial architectural style. With a terrace high above the park. It is especially pleasant to spend the evening here.

The other interesting sights are almost all near the park. To take a walking tour of the city, the right shoes and the right time of day are important. The best time is late afternoon. The city was built on a series of hills meaning there are numerous steep inclines. The humid heat of midday can prove exhausting. The following sights are somewhat farther from the park:

Moncada Military Fortress, entre Carretera Central y Calle Trinidad. During the dictatorship the Mancada military fortress was the second largest base in Cuba and a symbol of oppression and terror. The bullet holes originating from the storm on this base on July 21, 1953 *(→History)* can still be seen all around the entrance. The attack was during the Carnival season and the rebels hoped to take the base by surprise. However, one of the units was well acquainted with the city and got caught up in the crowds celebrating carneval. The attack failed.

Today the military fortress is a school. A museum provides information on the days of the dictatorship through photos, sketches and personal documents bringing the attack on the fortress to life. The fortress is open Monday from 8 am to 10 pm and Sunday from 8 am to noon.

Cementerio Santa Ifigenia, Avenida de las Americas. This is the second most beautiful cemetery in Cuba after the Columbus Cemetery in Havana. The ornate gravesites of Martí and Céspedes are especially worth seeing here. One can already see the Martí mausoleum from the entrance to the cemetery.

Castillo del Morro and the Pirate Museum. The full name of this fortification is "Castillo de San Pedro de la Roca" and it is situated high above the entrance to the bay on a limestone cliff. This vantage point provides a fantastic view of the Bay of Santiago and the Caribbean Sea. The museum inside offers information on the pirate attacks. Take the 211 departing from Calle Felix Pena near Parque Céspedes.

Santiago de Cuba / **Practical Information**
Accommodation

Las Américas, Avenida de las Américas y General Cebreco, Tel: 8040 or 8094; double rooms from $29 (£17). All rooms have a bathroom and toilet, radio, telephone and air conditioning. Restaurant, bar and swimming pool.

Balcón de Caribe, Careterra del Morro, Tel: 6561, 7 kilometres (4 miles) outside of town on a hilltop overlooking the city. Double rooms start at $27 (£16). Restaurant, bar and swimming pool. Rooms equipped like those in Las Américas.

Verasalles Altura de Versalles, 4 kilometres (2 miles) outside of town, the best but also the most expensive hotel in the city. Restaurant, bar, swimming pool, discotheque, tennis courts. All rooms like those above but with television and a refrigerator. Prices start at $60 (£36).

Leningrado, Carretera Siboney y Avenida Manduley, Tel: 20923. Spend the night in a pompous present from Moscow from around $30 (£18). Restaurant, bar, cafeteria, discotheque; all rooms like those in *Las Américas.*

Motel Rancho Club, Carretera Central toward Havana 4 kilometres (2 miles) out of town; double rooms from $22 (£13). Restaurant, bar, discotheque, swimming pool; room like those listed above.

Casa Grande, Parque de Céspedes; priced from $32 (£19). One cannot get more central than in this old colonial building. However, this hotel is no longer offered by *Cubatur* and the rooms are most often rented out to Cubans. One can still try at the reception desk despite this; western tourists do sometimes get a room.

Inexpensive Hotels (All in the centre of town)

Rex, Avenida Garzon;

Libertad, Calle Aguilera;

Imperial, Calle Sanchez y Felix Pena;

Venus, near Parque de Céspedes.

When booking one of these hotels (it is difficult), one does not go to the *Cubatur* office in *Casa Grande,* but to the new office to the right of the hotel. Ask directly for one of these hotels.

Activities

Casa Natal de José Maria Heredia, Calle Heredia, entre Hartmann y Pio Rosado. This is the house where the most famous lyricist was born – he was simultaneously politically active and was forced to spend most of his life in exile – is often the backdrop for cultural events.

Casa de la Trova, Calle Heredia, No. 208, just a short distance from the above. The Casa de la Trova originates from the 18th century. The door is always open. The famous troubadours almost constantly sing and dance their ballads in the small, dark room inside – the emotional *trovas* for which Santiago is so renowned. The room is usually filled to overflowing with a number of spectators standing in the streets surrounding the building.

Calle Heredia. Even on the street itself, there is often something going on. Once a month, the "noche cultural", the cultural night, takes place. Then, magicians, clowns, and puppeteers demonstrate their talent; troubadours and orchestras play and both young and old dance into the wee hours of the morning. The fantastic atmosphere should not be missed. One can ask when the next one is scheduled at the hotel reception or in the tourist information office on the ground floor of the *Casa Grande* Hotel.

Avenida Jesus Menendez: simply because of the numerous old carriages which roll up and down this street is the Avenida along the harbour definitely worth a stroll. In addition, this is also the location of the rum factory and cigar factory.

Art Galleries

Galería de UNEAC ("Union de Escritores y Artistas Cubanas"), Esq. Saco y San Augustin, Casa de la Amistad, Masó (San Basilio), entre Pio Rosado y Hartmann.

Galería de Arte de Oriente, Calle Lacret No. 656, entre Aguilera y Heredia.

SANTIAGO DE CUBA

Legend
1. St. Dolores Square and Church
2. Abel Santamaria Museum
3. Moncada Military Fortress
4. Interprovincial Bus Terminal
5. Zoo
6. Céspedes Park
7. Cancy Rum Factory
8. Santa Ifigenie Cemetery
9. Casa Natal de Antonio Maceo
10. Frank País Museum

Carneval

Santiago's Carneval is more ethnic and original than that in Havana. It is a typical street carnival without any pompous floats but dozens of bands and dance groups. Trumpets, piccolos, violins and foremost the congas never seem to miss a beat and transform the city centre into a churning cauldron (→*Holidays and Celebrations*).

Excursions

There are numerous destinations for excursions into the surrounding regions. However: a tour on one's own to discover these regions will require patience and a command of the language. The public transportation is poor. During the weekends, buses are filled to overflowing because just about everyone heads for the beach to swim. Finding a taxi for a longer trip into the surrounding regions is a matter of luck because many of the drivers do not like to drive that far from the city. The easiest and least strenuous way is to take advantage of what *Cubatur* offers. The office at Parque de Céspedes organises excursions to Gran Piedra National Park with →*La Isabelica*, to →*Granjita Siboney* and to →*Segundo Frente* near Mayári Arriba in the Sierra Cristal.

Those who would still rather take the bus should best take the No. 1 from Calle Aguilera near Parque Céspedes to the "Terminal de Omnibus Municipales". From here, the 14 goes to *Granjita Siboney* and to *Playa Siboney*. From Granjita, one can try to catch a bus up to *Gran Piedra*.

It is best but unfortunately also the most expensive to rent a car. If the expenses can be divided among several people, then the costs remain within limits.

Segundo Frente, Mayári Arriba. Near Mayári Arriba in the Sierra Cristal, Fidél Castro built up the so-called "second front" in February of 1958. The dictator answered by destroying numerous villages in the nearby regions. Posters and a small exhibition located here documents these events.

Cayo Granma. The small island lies in the Bay of Santiago de Cuba. Those who do not have a car should best take a taxi there. The long distance to the storybook island is definitely worthwhile: there doesn't seem to be a more beautiful place on earth than here. Many of the 1,500 residents only leave the island to go to work. Even the crossing with the ferry is an experience in itself. Also very much worth seeing is a *prehistoric valley,* which lies on the road from Santiago de Cuba via Granjita Siboney heading toward the sea. It was created by a Cuban artist and extends along both sides of the roadway. Various types of dinosaurs can be seen. One gains an impression of how this valley might have looked many years ago.

Around 2 kilometres (1 mile) farther are an *Automobile Museum* and a *Doll Museum.* In the Automobile Museum one can see everything from old-timers to toy cars. Some of these are real collectors items and rarities.

Museums

Casa Diego Velázquez (Colonial Museum), Parque de Céspedes. Open Monday to Saturday from noon to 3 pm; Sunday from 8 am to noon and 2 to 6 pm.

Museo "Abel Santamaria", Calle Trinidad y Carretera Central. Abel Santamaria was a close friend of Fidél Castro's and lost his life after the unsuccessful attack on the military base, having been tortured to death. Open Monday to Saturday from 8 am to noon and 2 to 6 pm; Sunday from 8:30 to noon and 6 to 8 pm.

Museo – Casa Natal de Frank y Josué Pais, Calle General Bandera No. 226 esq. Habana Los Maceos. Frank Pais was the leader and coordinator of the M-26, the movement of July 26, in operation in Santiago during the 1950s. On July 30, 1957, he was killed in a shootout with the police. His brother Josué had already been killed a month prior. Open Monday from 2 to 6 pm, Tuesday to Saturday from 8 am to noon and 2 to 6 pm.

Museo "Emilio Bacardi", Calle Pio Rosado, entre Heredia y Aguilera. This museum built in the neoclassicistic style in 1899 displays archaeological finds from the pre-Columbian period and documents from the wars of independence with Spain. The upper storey houses works by contemporary painters from this region. Open Monday from 2 to 8 pm, Tuesdays to Saturdays from 8 am to 2:45 pm and 3 to 8 pm, Sundays from 10 am to 4 pm.

Night Life: *Cabaret San Pedro del Mar,* Carretera del Morro, 7 kilometres (4 miles) outside of town next to the Hotel *Balcón de Caribe.* The best night club in this area.

Hotel *Las Américas,* Avenida de Las Américas.

Hotel *Versalles,* Altura de Versalles, 4 kilometres (2 miles) out of town.

Restaurants: The tourist hotels all have good restaurants. In the city itself, the best places to eat are:

Santiago 1900, Calle San Basilio, corner of Pio Rosado y Hartmann. Cuban and international cuisine served in a pleasant atmosphere with live table-side music.

Restaurant *El Baturro,* near the Parque Céspedes. Tasty chicken and pork dishes.

Restaurant *El Bodegon,* corner of Plaza de Dolores and Calle Aguilera. Dining like that in the famous *Bodeguita del Medio* (→Havana).

Restaurant *Punta Gorda,* across from Cayo Granma, 4 kilometres (2 miles) outside town. A cozy restaurant overlooking the bay. Speciality: seafood.

The average price for a meal in all of these restaurants is around 15 pesos. One can eat more inexpensively at:

Café Isabelica, Plaza de Dolores.

Pizzeria Italiana *El Galetto,* corner of Trocha y Avenida Ed. Chibas.

Pizzeria Italiana *Las Pirámides,* corner of Paseo Martí y René ramos Latour.

Casa de Té, Parque de Céspedes.

Shopping

The main shopping streets are the Heredia, Aguilera and José Saco.

Tourist Information

Cubatur, Casa Grande, Parque Céspedes, Tel: 7278.

Transportation *Air Travel:* There are daily flights to *Havana.* All other cities have several flights per week. One should take a taxi to the airport

Bus: The "Terminal de Omnibus Intermunicipales" is located on Carretera Central at the corner of Avenida de Los Libertadores and Calle 4 and offers service to →Guantánamo and Manzanillo among other cities.

The "Terminal de Omnibus Interprovinciales" is somewhat farther on the corner of Avenida de Los Libertadores and Calle 9. From here, buses depart direct to Havana – be sure and make reservations in advance.

The municipal bus no. 1 operates from Calle Aguilera near Parque Céspedes to these bus terminals, somewhat outside of town.

Bus no. 14 goes to the Playa Siboney beach from Avenida de Los Libertadores across from the "Hospital de la Maternidad".

The "Estación de Transporte Serrano" on Avenida de Los Libertadores across from the train station provides service to the villages in the Sierra Maestra.

Taxi: It is best to order a taxi at the hotel.

Collective Taxis: There are taxi stands at the "Terminal de Omnibus Intermunicipales". The trip to Guantánamo costs around 10 pesos.

Train: The "Estación de Ferrocariles" lies on the harbour. Trains depart daily for Havana and Guantánamo.

Shopping

Cuba is not a shoppers paradise. The revolution did provide the citizens with a certain level of affluence however, there is often scarcity regarding consumer goods. What the country does produce or import is usually required by its own population. The tourists are offered a number of things. The national tourist organisation Intur operates shopping centres in all of the hotels, bungalow complexes in which visitors can shop duty free. Among those articles offered are of course the world famous Cuban cigars and the obligatory rum. In addition there are tee shirts, jeans, records and cassettes, stuffed crocodiles and fetish dolls. For the "revolution tourists" there is a wide spectrum of tacky but interesting Che-Guevara-Kitsch including posters, rum glasses, chess games and lollipops – one will be confronted with the popular revolutionary almost everywhere.

Cubans are not allowed into the shops. Their frustration is understandable considering all of the high tech equipment offered by Sony and Akai. It is especially the young Cubans who ask the tourists if they would make some purchases for them in the Intur shops *(→Currency Regulations and Exchange)*. One should definitely take the precaution of making out a gift certification document if buying a larger number of items for Cubans. The Cubans are not allowed to be in the possession of any US dollars and this enforced with a prison sentence means they will accept these "presents" in secret. On the other hand in all of the other shops and restaurants in the cities not so heavily frequented by tourists one will pay in Cuban pesos. Most of the basic commodities are reserved for the Cubans by presenting a "libreta", a

Steep coastlines and rock formations are typical of Cuba's coastal regions in addition to its numerous sandy beaches

rations card. There are markets with "free sales" (venta libre). Here the tourists can also purchase bread and fruit depending on the supply.

In Havana in addition to the above mentioned shopping for tourists there are two special boutiques in the embassy districts of Miramar, the "La Maison" and the "La Flora". What is offered is similar to that in the Intur shops but the quality of the textiles is much better. In "La Maison" there is also a very nice swimming pool and a pleasant cafeteria.

When paying with travellers cheques in a shop change is given in US dollars.

Sights

Cuba maintains and preserves its cultural heritage. Not only the achievements of the Cuban revolution (kindergartens, schools, hospitals, research institutes) are proudly shown to visitors and included on Cubatur tours, but also the remnants from the Spanish colonial period are carefully restored and presented to the public – that is if finances allow for this. One good example of this is the "Cultural Monument of Humanity" which is what the old city districts of Havana and Trinidad were declared – Cuba's colonial treasure chest.

The revolutionary government placed great value on the political education of its citizens. Every city and almost even every village has a museum or a monument commemorating the events during the past one hundred years and explaining the historical context which lead to the revolution of 1959. Cuban archaeologists have meticulously collected the aritifacts from the erradicated native Indian population and put them on display in museums as well.

Of course, the Cuban landscapes are also worth seeing: the Oriente and the Okzidente of the island are especially attractive with rugged mountain ranges, dense cedar and mahogony forests, idyllic villages in palm groves and the white beaches lining the island's coast. This is to say that Cuba has just as much to offer those interested in culture as it does to nature lovers.

Soroa

The resort town of Soroa lies 80 kilometres (50 miles) west of Havana in the Sierra Rosario mountains. Earlier, the entire region was owned by a certain Don Ignatio Soroa, who mainly farmed coffee.

The sulfer baths in this town attract numerous people from Havana. The actual attraction of Soroa is, however, its orchid gardens. Over 700 orchid species are bred in the gardens which cover an area of 35,000 square metres (374,252 square feet) – a treat to the eye as well as the nose. Located near the *Orquideario* is the holiday complex of *Villa Turistica Soroa*. From here, a small footpath leads up to the *Miraflores* scenic overlook at an elevation of 500 metres (1,650 feet). During clear weather, one can see both the northern and southern coasts of Cuba from here. Below the villa, a pathway winds through a small forest comprising carob trees and spruce down to *Salto de Soroa*, Soroa's waterfall. It is possible to swim in the natural pool at the base.

Accommodation: *Villa Turistica Soroa,* all rooms with a bathroom and air conditioning. This complex, somewhat run-down in appearance, has a restaurant, a cafeteria, a discotheque and a swimming pool. Double rooms are priced from $32 (£19).

Telephones

Telephone connections between Cuba and the rest of the world function best at the post office in the *Habana Libre* Hotel *(→Havana/Practical Information).*

Tipping

Tipping is no longer customary in Cuba but is still discretely accepted in some places – this, a result of the growing tourism industry. It is a more elegant option, however, to ask the personnel if they might enjoy something from the Intur shop.

Tourist Season

Cuba's climate is warm and humid during the entire year. The average annual temperature is 25°C(77°F). The best time to visit Cuba arriving from Europe is during the Cuban "winter" from December to April. One can swim in the Ocean any time of year. During July and August, Cubans have their holidays. In addition, July is the Carnival season. During these times, just about everyone floods to the beaches and carvinal cities of Havana and Santiago de Cuba.

Traffic Regulations

Cars drive on the right-hand side of the road in Cuba. Traffic signs and regulations are about the same as those in Europe or North America. The island has a total of 11,746 kilometres (7,341 miles) of roadway in good to very good condition. There are paved roads to all of the points of interest to tourists.

The Cuban drivers are spirited, but disciplined. Also, the condition of their vehicles usually does not allow for high speeds. Turn signals do not always function; in these cases, one merely uses hand signals. One should slow down when approaching railway crossings since the rails often protrude above the asphalt quite a ways. Traffic lights are not always in operation making the horn the most important piece of equipment on the car.

Travel Documents

Since Cuba has opened for tourism, entering the country has been made a lot easier. Those who do not plan on staying in the country for more than 72 hours, need at least proof of a hotel reservation. Those who plan on staying in Cuba longer will need a tourist card.

Tourist Cards

Visitors who have booked a package tour receive a tourist card together with the other papers in the travel agency. The card must be given back to the travel agent filled out in its entirity then sent for approval at one of the Cubatur offices. Both carbon copies must be kept in a safe place and simply must be presented with a passport when entering the country.

Those travelling individually must specifcally request a tourist card from the agent booking their flight. It is less expensive to get this at a Cuban embassy. Important for those travelling on their own: besides their travel card and their passports they must have proof of a hotel reservation for at least two nights when entering the country. Without this confirmation the customs officials will deny entry. However, there is the possibility of making these reservations at the airport in Havana →*Havana* in the Cubaturs office there. Here one can save the administration fee that is usually charged at travel agents at home. The catch is however that this office usually offers the most expensive accommodation in Havana with the freindly remark that all of the inexpensive hotels were booked. Thus, those who have not yet made a booking will be given a room in the very luxurious *Habana Riviera (→Travelling in Cuba/Cubatur and Intur)*. The tourist cards are valid for four weeks and must be stamped by the first hotel on one's travel itinerary. It is possible to have the validity extended by the Cubatur office for individual tourists in Hotel Habana Libre in Havana if one has proof of additional hotel reservations.

Visas

Those who are not on holiday but on business in Cuba must apply for a visa either at the Cuban Embassy or Consulate or at the Cubatur office. In addition, most travel agents will be able to help with these formalities.

Driving Licence

The national driving licence issued at home is in most cases sufficient when renting a car. The minimum age for renting a car is 21 years of age.

Travel in Cuba

Travel in Cuba / **Cubatur and Intur**

The state operated tourism organisation called Cubatur arranges just about everything from reserving a table in restaurants and nightclubs, hotel and holiday village reservations, theatre tickets, domestic flight tickets to excursions to the old colonial cities as well as arranging for rental cars. There is a *Cubatur Information desk* in all of the tourist hotels (open from 10 am to 7 pm),

Buying snacks on the streets - a scene reminiscent of Graham Greene's era

and also an office in the larger towns and cities.

In smaller towns, it is usually the " Institute for National Tourism", *Intur* which will be able to help tourists. For those travelling on their own, the *Information Office for Individual Tourism* in the *Habana Libre* Hotel has been in existence since 1985. This office helps in planning travel routes and books hotels and flights.

In Havana, the Cubatur office is on the "Rampa", Calle 23, No. 156, Ciudad de Habana 4; Tel: 32-4521, Telex TURCU 511 243.

Other Cubatur offices worldwide include: Cubatur, 440 Boulevard Dorchester Ouest, Suite 1402, Montréal Canada, Tel: (514) 857-8004; Cubatur55 Queen Street East, Suite 705, Toronto Canada, Tel: (416) 362-0700; Cubatur, Insurgentes Sur 421 y Aguascalientes, Complejo Aristos, Edificio B, Local 310, México DF 060100, Tel: 574-9454; Cubatur, 24 rue de 4 Septembre, F-75002 Paris France, Tel: 7 42 54 15; Cubatur, Steinweg 2, D-60313 Frankfurt am Main Germany, Tel: (069) 28 83 22.

The best way to escape the heat of the cities is out on the water

Travel in Cuba / **Means of Transportation**

Those who want to discover more of Cuba have the choice between a number of means of transportation, including special tourist buses and taxis and the public transportation. When using public transportation, one will however, require patience, good physical condition, a sense of adventure and foremost sufficient Spanish skills.

Tourist Buses and Taxis

This transportation service is only available in Havana and Varadero at present. From these two cities, there are excursions to all areas of interest. For reservations, contact the tourist offices in the larger hotels, or Cubatur. In front of the entrances to tourist hotels are tourist taxis which can be easily recognised, by the large T on the doors. If planning on visiting points of interest outside of Havana advance booking is necessary. In doing this it is better to go to a hotel with tourist taxis personally rather than making a reservation by telephone. It is very important to give exact dates and times for trips to the airport since there is not yet a shuttle service there *(→Havana)*.

Municipal Buses

The least expensive way to discover the city is to use the municipal buses. Making sure one is seated on the correct bus is, however, not that simple. There are no bus schedules. At least in Havana, in the *Habana Libre* and *Nacional* Hotels there are bus schedules posted for buses to the old city. However, the visitors will most often end up having to ask their way around. If one has successfully the right "parada" (bus stop) then one must stand in line. Each new person to arrive always asks: "El último?" (the last). The price on the bus trip is 5 centavos which is deposited into the metal container next to the driver. Those who would like to get off the bus but are blocked off from the exit by a crowd of people should shout out "Parada" hit the roof of the bus and make their way to the door calling out "permeso" ("excuse me").

Cross-Country Buses

Cross-country buses are inexpensive. It is exactly for this reason that they are probably the most frequently used means of transportation in Cuba. Demand is high and capacity is not always sufficient. Information, reservation services and tickets are available at the "Reservaciones de Omnibus Nacionales" Offices or directly at the bus terminals. It is necessary to reserve a seat as soon as possible.

There are different types of buses. The "especiales" are air conditioned, faster and more comfortable than the "regulares", which can be quite exhausting when covering long distances. When the buses run to different provinces they are called "interprovinciales"; for service to other towns and cities within a given province, "provinciales" or "intermunicipales"; and "locales" when they offer service to villages within a given municipality.

At the bus terminal, one will receive a waiting number ("numero de espera") with the bus ticket. This is to regulate the order in which the passengers board the bus. There is a waiting list ("lista de espera") posted in the waiting area with all of the numbers. One can then see approximately where one is in line. It is recommended to arrive at the terminal at least one hour before departure, otherwise the seats are given to someone else.

Taxis

Generally speaking, there are taxi stands in front of every hotel and near bus terminals, railway stations and airports; taxis can also be ordered through a central taxi station. For this reason they do not stop for hand signals even if they have no passengers. Only on the return trip will they pick up passengers; therefore, *always* wave when spotting a taxi. The fare is registered on a taximeter and payment is expected in pesos. The base price is 50 centavos and each kilometre costs 25 centavos. At night after 2 am, each kilometre costs 30 centavos. For tourists there are special tourist taxis which are marked with a T on the door. Payment for these is made in US dollars. In addition to the taxis, there are "maquinas", maintained by the drivers, these offer collective taxi service on set routes to a large number of places, often offering shuttle service between cities. They wait as long as it takes to fill all the seats. "Maquinas" are less expensive than taxis since the fare is divided among all passengers.

Train Travel: The railway through Cuba is from Guantánamo in the east to Guane in the west. There are four types of trains: " servicio especial", "primera especial", "segunda especial", and finally the "lechero", slower trains called the "milkman". The only one to provide service between Havana and Santiago de Cuba is the "servicio especial". It is equipped with a cafeteria wagon and takes 15 to 20 hours to cover this route making it a viable alternative (also in terms of price) to the cross-country buses. At best, the night express will take 15 hours, but one must expect delays.

For first class trains, advance reservations are necessary. To reserve a seat, one must go to one of two large train stations in Havana. One hour before the departure (but two hours are better) one must reconfirm the reservation. Otherwise the tickets are sold to other passengers.

Air Travel: The only relatively reliable means of transportation in Cuba are the flights. Planes depart from Havana to every larger city on the island. The same rule of thumb is true for air travel as well: demand is high so make reservations early. Tickets can be purchased at the *Cubana de Aviación* office at the Calle 23 near the "Rampa" or at the Office for Individual Tourism in the

Habana Libre Hotel. Payment is accepted in US dollars or pesos when presenting a currency exchange receipt. The return trip from Havana to Santiago de Cuba costs around $50 (£30). Other destinations include: →*Baracoa*, →*Bayamo*, →*Camagüey*, →*Cienfuegos*, →*Guantánamo*, →*Holguín*, Manzanillo, Moa, Niquero, Las Tunas and →*Santa Clara*.

Travelling to Cuba

Tourists from western countries come to Cuba by air almost without exception. However, before taking the trip, one should definitely consider the best possible way to see what the island has to offer. There are three alternatives:

1. Group travel with a set itinerary: the traditional way to get to know this "red" island. The participants, are still guided as revolutionary tourists, get to know the country in a short time focussing on culture and language, politcs and science, and the education and health system. Supplementing this are Cubas beautiful beaches offering fantastic conditions for aquatic sports or simply for a relaxing time. The tour organisers generally have years of experience of Cuba and employ travel guides with a good knowledge of the country and the language.

2. Package Tours

Since the beginning of the 1980s, Cuba has also been incorporated into the tours offered by the larger organisations. They offer everything from a week in Havana and Varadero, to three week itineraries with full board, tour of the islands and a visit to the beaches. It is customary for the traveller to put together his own itinerary from the large range offered. The differences in price and value however are enormous; comparing what each company has to offer might be worthwhile. One thing that can be said is that a trip to Cuba comprising weeks only visiting the beaches is relatively inexpensive.

3. Travelling Individually

In the last few years Cuba has been opened up to those travelling on their own. Anyone can now visit the island as an individual tourist, a good road network connects all the places worth seeing, although the system is sometimes stubborn the transport system is functional.

Travelling on your own is an exciting and lasting experience especially for Cuba. However, one should critically consider the following thoughts before planning ones trip:

The colonial era has left its unmistakable mark on Cuba's architecture

1. Those who want to forego travelling in groups should have at least a good knowledge of Spanish to use in banks and hotels, in shops, at bus stops, and reading signs... everything is in Spanish. One is better off not assuming that someone will speak English and what is more annoying than getting accustomed to the country is the fact that ones oppurtunities to meet and converse with the Cubans are limited if one does not have a command of the language. (→Languages).

2. Those who are used to cooking for themselves on a trip will certainly have problems in Cuba. Department stores and shops are scarce and the special prices are reserved for the Cubans who are given "libretas " to purchase these products. For a number of years however there have been markets with no selling restrictions, offering fruits and vegetables. Markets, however, are not a reliable source for these products since they are dependent on supplies from the surrounding region. Ultimately, one can usually purchase groceries – usually canned goods – in the state-run Intur Shops located in the tourist hotels. Otherwise, the individual travellers should be prepared to eat in the restaurants and sleep in the hotels. There are no youth hostels nor are there any private guest houses (→Accommodation). This should all be taken into account when calculating ones holiday budget.

It is difficult for the individual tourist to arrange tours of sugar and tabacco factories as well as educational institutions and hospitals, since these tours are conceived for travel groups. Sightseeing tours for package trips are operated by Cubatur (→Travel in Cuba), the state run tourism organisation. In individual cases it is possible to take part in such a tour. More information is available at the Cubatur office.

3. It is very important to book hotel rooms, restaurants and transport before arriving in Cuba. Without this foresight, there is little on offer after arrival in Cuba, even though a glance over the receptionists shoulder will show that there are rooms available. Although it is meanwhile possible to get a hotel room after having arrived in Cuba it is still the better option to work out a travel route at home and book all of the hotel rooms that will be needed along the way in advance. Quite often the hotels one would like to stay in are completely booked on short notice. The booking system also makes it difficult to be more flexible along a given travel route.

Trinidad

Trinidad was founded in 1514 and is Cuba's colonial jewel. Since the modern development at the end of the 19th century passed over Trinidad leaving it virtually untouched, the Spanish colonial city could be preserved to present unchanged. Today, this city with a population of 35,000 is one of the excursion destinations offered by *Cubatur.*

Trinidad / **History**

The first Spanish settlers lived from panning for gold in the nearby Río Tayabo. The fold in this river was, however, quickly depleted and the residents focussed their attention on smuggling, which flourished well into the 17th century. As was the case with Cuba's other cities, Trinidad also had to contend with the pirate attacks during this time. Beginning in the mid 18th century, sugar cane and the slave trade became the main sources of income. A propertied bourgeois class developed, the fantastic affluence of which made a luxurious lifestyle possible. One hundred years later, 40 sugar factories around Trinidad produced approximately 17 million pounds of sugar annually. When the sugar prices ultimately fell, the hundred years of affluence came to an abrupt end and competition from the up-and-coming city of Cienfuegos did the rest in forcing Trinidad into poverty, making the city insignificant almost overnight. Today, many call Trinidad the "city of had's" since some of its white residents still enjoy talking about their ancestors who "had" power and wealth.

Trinidad / **Sights**

There are no really outstanding individual sights in Trinidad – a stroll through the cobblestone streets and alleyways is the best way to gain an impression of the atmosphere of days gone by, which is indeed the main attraction of this city, rich in history. There are only a few cars but all the more horse-drawn carts and donkeys which often provide transportation for a number of generations. The most beautiful area is the district north of Calle Martí, surrounding *Plaza Mayor.* For many, this square is Cuba's most beautiful. It is bordered by the palaces which once belonged to the city's creme de la creme. Beyond the plaza toward *Iglesia de la Papa,* a short walk leads through narrow alleyways up to this church from the 17th century. From here, one has a magnificent view of the Caribbean Sea.

Trinidad / **Practical Information**
Accommodation
Hotels
Hotel Ancon, Playa Ancon. A large but not very pretty hotel. All rooms are equipped with the standard facilities: a bathroom, toilet, air conditioning and radio. There are restaurants, bars, a discotheque, a cafeteria, shops and boutiques in the hotel. Double rooms start at $34 (£20).
Costa Sur, Playa Ancón; double rooms start at $20 (£12). All rooms with bath and toilet, air conditioning and radio. Restaurant, bar and swimming pool.

Motel *Las Cuevas*, in the mountains northeast of the city. A fantastic view of Trinidad and the Caribbean Sea. Good restaurant; rooms furnished like those in *Costa Sur;* double rooms from $27 (£16).

Hotel *Siboney*, Calle Martí near Parque Céspedes. An inexpensive hotel in the centre of town with double rooms priced from 10 pesos.

Hotel *Canada*, Calle Martí, from 10 pesos.

Hotel *Ronda*, next to Hotel Canada, around 5 pesos.

Camping

Base Manacal, 6 kilometres (4 miles) outside the city in the mountains; rather secluded. Suited for those cooking their own meals.

Playa Ancón, 2 kilometres (1 miles) from Hotel *Costa Sur.* This camping area rents out tents and meals are served in the hotels. There is also a cafeteria on the camping grounds.

One monument follows the next in Havana's "Parque de la Fraternidad", the "Park of Brotherhood"

Excursions

Topes Collantes. A recreation area 20 kilometres (12 miles) outside the city on the slopes of the Sierra del Escambray. Numerous hiking paths lead through cedar and pine forests along the azure blue backdrop of the Caribbean sea, lying 800 metres (2,616feet) lower. This area offers peace and relaxation. Accommodation: Hotel *Los Pinos,* double rooms priced around $30 (£18): Restaurant, horseback riding.

Hotel Kurotel Topes Collantes in the Sanatorium: luxurious with Cuban art in the rooms and corridors. From $31 (£19) for a double room.

Insider Tip: Truck rides and hiking through the jungle regions, swimming at the base of waterfalls. $30 (£18) from Hotel *Ancón,* $25 (£15) from Hotel *Topes Collantes.* Ask for Guanayara or the guides Jorge and Martinez. One can also *Hotel Los Helechos:* inexpensive and clean; double rooms from $21 (£13).

Torre Iznaga, 14 kilometres (9 miles) outside of the city toward Sancti Spíritus. This tower was built at the beginning of the 19th century by the Iznaga family. Originally, it stood in the middle of a huge sugar plantation. The slaves could be patrolled from this perch – an oppressive symbol of the unlimited power of the sugar barons at that time.

The "Castillo de los Tres Reyes" counts among the oldest Spanish fortifications in the New World

Valle de los Ingenios. The "Valley of the Sugar Mills" lies 4 kilometres (2 miles) before Trinidad and offers a breathtaking sight. At the beginning of the 19th century, 48 sugar mills stood here and there are still some ruins among the palms and fruit trees.

Museums

The following museums are located on Plaza Mayor:

Museo Romántico

In the former Palacio Brunet, the furnishings belonging to upper-class families from Trinidad during the early 19th century are on display. The building itself originates from the 18th century. Open Tuesday to Saturday from 9 am to noon and 2 to 6 pm; Sunday from 2 to 6 pm.

Museo de Arquitectura Trinitaria

This small museum offers insight into the old, local methods of construction with stone and clay.

Museo de Arqueologia Guamuhaya

The building can be recognised by its balcony which runs around the entire building. The museum displays finds from the pre-Columbian era. Among these is an Indian grave dating back around 2,000 years. Open Tuesday to Saturday from 8 am to noon and 2 to 6 pm, Sunday from 8 am to noon.

Museo de Alejandro de Humboldt

As the first universally educated German, Alexander von Humboldt arrived in Trinidad in March of 1801 and stayed longer than he had planned due to the interesting landscape in which he observed, collected and wrote.

The Museum of Natural History is dedicated to him and exhibits stuffed, slightly dusty animals from this region – among them a sea-cow. Open Tuesday to Saturday from 8 am to noon and 2 to 6 pm, Sunday from 8 am to noon.

Museo de la Lucha Contra Bandidos

The museum lies on Calle Bolívar and provides information on the battles against the counterrevolutionaries called the "bandits" who operated from the Escambray mountains during the 1960s. The information provided is in the form of photos and documents.

Restaurants

Restaurante *Las Cuevas,* in the Motel with the same name above the city.

Inexpensive cafeterias and pizzerias can be found in the city along Calle Martí.

Tourist Information

Cubatur, Calle Martí, entre Calle Cienfuegos y Lino Perez, Tel: 2554, near Parque Céspedes.

Transportation
The bus terminal is on Calle Güinart. Buses depart from here into the surrounding regions as well as to Cienfuegos, Sancti Spíritus and Havanna (→individual entries).

Vaccinations →Medical Care

Varadero

Even after the revolution, Varadero remains Cuba's premiere beach resort. Its 20 kilometres (12 miles) of white sandy beaches brought it world renown and even millionaires from North America prized this city for that very reason. During those times, the entire city was privately owned. Cubans, especially those with dark complexions, were denied entry. Their pompous luxury villas have meanwhile been renovated and converted into hotels; modern hotel complexes were added. The beach is now, of course, open to the public. Located 140 kilometres (88 miles) from Havana, Varadero is now the largest tourist centre in Cuba and a synonym for a relaxing holiday on the beach.

Varadero / **Practical Information**
Accommodation
There are numerous accommodations in Varadero. However, these are not all inexpensive and payment is only accepted in US dollars. Among the hotels are those in old villas, one camping area and modern tourist complexes. The latter all lie north of the old city centre and are reminiscent of the less than beautiful tourist architecture along some sections of the Mediterranean coast. Reservations are mandatory. Finding a satisfactory hotel spontaneously is difficult. One option might be to book a more expensive hotel through Cubatur for a few days and look for something more appropriate from there.

Hotels Hotel Internacional, Avenida de las Américas, Tel: 553-260 or 3011; around $60 (£36). All rooms with air conditioning, bathroom and toilet, radio and television. Located directly on the beach. There is a swimming pool, several restaurants, a cafeteria, Intur shops and a good bar with live music.

Hotel Kawama, Camino del Mar, entre Calle 0 y Calle 1, Tel: 3173 or 63113; double rooms are priced from $61 (£37). Directly on the beach; small bungalows all equipped with bathroom and toilet, air conditioning, telephone, radio and television. There is a restaurant, a bar, shopping and numerous sports facilities.

Hotel Atabey, Calle 60 y Autopista, Tel: 63012. The same style as Atabey, 400 yards to the beach, priced from $63 (£38).

Hotel Oasis, Via Blanca, Tel: 2902 or 62902, somewhat off from the entrance to town; priced from $51 (£30). Equipped the same as Siboney but with a pool.

Hotel Bellamar, Calle 17, entre 1 y 2, Tel: 63012, from $63 (£38). 200 yards to the sea but furnished with the typical American "motel-look". Rooms furnished as in Atabey.

Hotel Pullman, Calle 49, Tel: 62575, a small hotel near the beach with double rooms starting at $28 (£17).

Hotel Ledo, Avenida Playa y 43; from $25 (£15). A simple hotel in the old city centre across from the cinema.

Hotel Marbella, 1. Avenida y 42; from $26 (£16).

Another inexpensive hotel is the *Hotel Tropical Astoria* on Avenida Playa; from $31 (£19).

Villas

Villa Arenas Blancas, Calle 64 y Avenida 1, Tel: 62358; from $40 (£24). Near the sea; all of the bungalows are air conditioned and equipped with bathroom and toilet, radio and television. Restaurant and bar, Intur shop.

Villa Caribe, Avenida de Playa y Calle 30, Tel: 6 33 10; from $35 (£21). Directly on the beach with a restaurant, bar and cafeteria. Rooms furnished like above.

Villa Cuba, Avenida de las Américas, Tel: 62975; from $40 (£24). Directly on the beach with a restaurant and bar.

Villa Tortuga, Calle 7, entre Avenida 1 y Mar, Tel: 62243 or 2243; from $35 (£21). Near the sea.

Villa Barlovento, Calle 11 y Mar, Tel: 63721; from $32 (£19). Directly on the beach with boat rental, restaurant and bar.

Villa Los Cocos, Calle 22 y Mar, Tel: 62552; from $32 (£19). Restaurant and bar.

Villa Los Delfines, Avenida Playa y Calle 39, Tel: 63305; from $32 (£19). Restaurant and bar.

Villa Solimar, Avenida de las Américas before the Hotel Internacional, Tel: 2217; from $43 (£26). Restaurant and cabaret.

Villa Sotavento, Calle 13 y Camino del Mar, Tel: 62953 or 2953; from $32 (£19). Restaurant and cabaret.

Villa Cuatro Palmas, Calle 59 y Mar, Tel: 62251 or 2251; from $31 (£18). Directly on the beach with a cozy restaurant.

Villa Herradura, Avenida Playa y Calle 36, Tel: 62648 or 2648; from $31 (£18). Directly on the beach with a restaurant, swimming pool and discotheque.

Camping

Centro Túristico Rincón Francés Camismó, northeast of the hotel complexes.

The Jagüey: a type of willow with its exposed aerial roots

Take the Bus with the sign for Las Morales from Varadero. The trip takes 30 minutes and buses depart every hour to Varadero. Accommodation in tents or wooden cottages with four beds from 15 pesos. There is no possibility to lock up one's belongings and if demand is high there is not always enough food. Subjective opinion: too far away and the furnishing and sanitary facilities leave room for improvement.

Activities During the Day

Naturally, sports and recreation concentrate on the water. Simply due to the heat, sports on land can be a very tiring endeavour.

Aquatic Sports: All of the large hotels offer scuba diving, snorkelling at the coral reef, surfing, fishing, rowing, water-skiing and sailing.

Golf: A United States millionaire by the name of Dupont had a golf course built east of Varadero. Today, it is open to the public. Three to four hours cost $10 (£6); open from 9 am to 5 pm.

Tennis: Hotels *Internacional, Bellamar* and *Kawama* as well as the Villas *Cabañas del Sol, Cuatro Palmas, Arenas Blancas, Los Cocos, Sotavento* and *Tortuga* have tennis courts. They are open from 9 am to 5 pm and tennis rackets and balls are available in the hotels.

Horseback Riding: Horses are rented out by Hotel *Oasis* and Villa *Cuba* Sunday to Friday from 9 am to 5 pm.

Most of the tourists find this all a bit too tiring and prefer to relax on the beach within the appropriate proximity to a beach bar. Palm covered bars with refrigerators are scattered at all of the strategic points on the beach making a stroll along the beach quite possibly into bar-hopping.

Excursions

The tourist offices in the hotels and holiday villages organise tours lasting one to several days to the Guamá crocodile farm, to the Tropicana in Havana, to Soroa orchid park and into the Viñales Valley, to Santa Clara, Hanabanilla and Trinidad *(→individual entries).*

Those who embark on excursions on their own should consider that they will need to plan in a couple of additional days.

Those who want to visit the scuba diving paradise of →*Cayo Largo* will not be able to avoid an organised excursion.

Museum

Varadero's history is documented in a house typical of the turn-of-the-century on Calle 57 y Avenida Playa.

Night Life

The night life is heavily influenced by the tourism. The wide selection of nightclubs and discotheques is not typical of the rest of Cuba.

Cabaret Continental (in the Hotel Internacional); Cuban live music and dancing; open Tuesday to Sunday from 8 pm to 3 am.

Cueva del Pirata, on the Autopista on the left-hand side after about 9 kilometres (5 miles). This cabaret is in a former pirate's cave, the waiters also wear the appropriate costumes. Cuban live music and pop music.

Discoteca La Rada, at the harbour near Via Blanca at kilometre marker 31. A meeting place for the younger croud, western and Latin American pop music. Open Tuesday to Sunday from 9 pm to 3 am.

Discoteca Sahara, in Hotel Oasis. Western and Latin American pop music. Open 8 pm to 3 am.

Discoteca La Patana, on an old ship in the lagoon. Western and Latin American pop music. Open Tuesday to Sunday from 8 pm to 3 am.

El Kastillo, Avenida Playa y Calle 49. Western and Latin American pop music. Open 8:30 pm to 3 am.

Restaurants

Most of the hotels and *villas* have a restaurant or cafeteria. One should make reservations for the following restaurants.

Las Américas, Avenida de las Américas y Autopista, in the northeast portion of the peninsula. This is Varadero's most expensive restaurant serving international cuisine. The personnel is often overtaxed when serving larger groups. Open from noon to 10 pm, closed Mondays.

The restaurant is housed in the ostentatious villa which once belonged to the wealthies man in the city. The US multi-millionaire Irenée Dupont de Nemours not only owned this land with a golf course and private runway for his jet but also numerous plots of land in Varadero. The valuable organ in this house is said to have only cost him one million dollars. 113 employees worked during the entire year in this villa even though Dupont himself only spent two weeks a year here. Today, the Dupont villa and its gardens is a recreation area for Cubans and foreign visitors.

Albacora, Calle 59 entre Avenida 1 y Mar, Tel: 63811; open Tuesday to Sunday from 3 to 11 pm, closed Mondays. Speciality of the house: seafood.

La Arcada, Villa Punta Blance; international cuisine; open 7:30 to 10 am (breakfast), noon to 5 pm (lunch), 7 to 10:15 pm (dinner).

El Bodegón Criollo, Avenida Playa y Calle 40, Tel: 62180. Creole cuisine in a relaxed atmosphere; open noon to midnight.

La Cabanita, Calle 9 y Avenida Playa; meat and fish dishes. Open 10 am to 1 am.

Special Events: Once a week, the hotels hold a "noche especiale" with shows with Cuban rhythms. In July and August, Varadero is in the throes of Carnival (→*Holidays and Celebrations*). Even tourists can take part in a dance com-

petition. In the cinemas "Cine Varadero" on Avenida Playa and the "Cine Hicacos" on Avenida 1 often have undubbed films in English.

The International Festival of Latin American Music takes place annually in the amphitheatre. This is the largest cultural event of this kind in Latin America.

Transportation: Cross-country buses depart from the "Estación de Omnibus Interprovinciales" on Avenida 1 y Calle 15. These provide service to all of the larger cities on the island.

Travelling from Havana

Bus: Departing from the "Terminal de Omnibus Interproviciales" in Vadedo, daily.

Collective Taxis: Departing from the corner of Gloria y Agramonte near Estación Central in Habana Vieja.

Tourist Taxis: Departing from Hotel *Havana Libre* in Vedado. Expensive!

Important Addresses: *Pharmacies:* Avenida Playa y Calle 44, open 24 hours. Avenida 1 y Calle 28; open 8 am to 11 pm. *Information: Cubatur,* Avenida 1, entre Calle 26 y 27.

Vegetation

Growing in Cuba are over 600 species of higher plants. It is true that the one crop economy based on sugar cane and the shipbuilding industry during the colonial era did leave only 8% of the land area for forests; however, there is still plenty for the amateur botanist to discover. One example are the delicate *cork palms* which can grow to a height in excess of 9 metres (30 feet) despite their thin trunks only 30 cm (12 inches) in diametre. Another is the mighty *royal palm,* Cuba's trademark. The *kapok tree* is easily recognised by its white trunk. The *jagüey* is similar to weeping willow, however, it is the roots that hang to the ground, absorbing nutrients from the air and not the leaves.

As coveted as ever are the valuable woods from the *yaya* the *cedar* and the *mahogany* trees. The most beautiful of the decorative trees is the *flamboyant* with its bright red blossoms. Other plants include *jacaranda bush, coral trees,* and the *Indian laburnum (golden chain tree). Mangoes, avocados,* and *papayas* count among the most widespread fruit trees. A feast for the eye and nose are the hundreds of *orchids* from →*Sarao* a small town in the Sierra del Rosario in the western portions of the island. The *Hibiscus* can be found in Cuba in almost every possible colour.

The Martí Mausoleum: a place of pilgrimage in honour of the revolutionary hero

Viñales

Viñales is a small village 25 kilometres (16 miles) north of Pinar del Río in one of Cuba's most beautiful landscapes. It was established in 1895 by tobacco farmers 200 kilometres (125 miles) from Havana.

The main attraction, however, is not the village but the valley in which it lies. Bizarre limestone cones called "mogotes" tower up from the valley basin. In early geological history, these served as the supporting columns for a type of "earthen roof" over the valley. At one point, this "roof" collapsed, leaving only the columns. Outside of the tobacco season, the farmers here cultivate the fast-growing yucca and malanga.

Viñales / **Sights**

For tourists, Viñales itself has little to offer. The main attraction, as stated above, is the valley which can, however, only be explored on foot along the main road.

El Mural de la Prehistoria, the "wall of prehistory". Spanning a length of over 200 metres (655 feet), the Cuban artist Leovigildo González has depicted the history of human development on a wall of the "Mogote Dos Hermanos" (accessible via a footpath from the village).

Cueva del Indio. A large cavern around 5 kilometres (3 miles) outside of Viñales. A dance bar has been set up inside the cave. One can wander through the entire length of this cave and leave the cave by way of boat on an underground river. The entrance is on the road to San Vicente and can be easily spotted thanks to its large parking area.

Bus Tour: Viñales – Pinar del Rio. This bus tour includes a meal, visits to a tobacco and a rum factory and costs $30 (£18) *(→Office for Individual Tourism* under *Travel in Cuba).*

Viñales / **Practical Information**

Accommodation: *Hotel Los Jazmines,* high above the valley on the road to Pinar del Río, Tel: 932197; double rooms from $26 (£15). The magnificent view makes this hotel in one of the best locations in Cuba. In addition to the view, this hotel offers a good restaurant and a swimming pool.

Motel *Rancho San Vicente,* San Vicente, somewhat neglected, with a restaurant, bar, discotheque and swimming pool; double rooms from $26 (£15).

Restaurant: *Cueva del Indio,* on the road to San Vicente; cozy and inexpensive.